Main Street Mirth

Main Street Mirth

INSPIRATIONAL STORIES,
QUOTES, AND QUIPS
FROM AROUND TOWN

Mary Hollingsworth
GENERAL EDITOR

Guideposts Books
CARMEL, NEW YORK

Copyright © 2006 by Guideposts, Carmel, New York 10512. All rights reserved.

Let There Be Laughter! is a trademark of Guideposts.

No part of this publication may be reproduced, stored in a retrieval system or transmitted in any form or by any means, electronic, mechanical, photocopying, recording or otherwise, without the written permission of the publisher. Inquiries should be addressed to the Rights & Permissions Department, Guideposts, 16 E. 34th St., New York, NY 10016.

Every attempt has been made to credit the sources of copyrighted material used in this book. If any such acknowledgment has been inadvertently omitted or miscredited, receipt of such information would be appreciated. Credit lines for all entries can be found in the back of this book.

All Scripture quotations, unless otherwise noted, are taken from The Holy Bible, New Century Version®, copyright © 1987, 1988, 1991 by Thomas Nelson, Inc. All rights reserved.

Scripture quotations marked (GNB) are from the *Good News Bible, The Bible in Today's English Version*. Copyright © American Bible Society, 1966, 1971, 1976.

Editorial, research, and content development managed by Shady Oaks Studio, Bedford, Texas. Team members: Patty Crowley, Vicki Graham, Rhonda Hogan, Mary Hollingsworth, Sue Ann Jones, Mary Kay Knox, Kathryn Murray, Nancy Norris, Stephany Stevens, Stephanie Terry, and Barbara Tork.

Produced in association with Mark Sweeney & Associates, Bonita Springs, Florida.

www.guideposts.org
(800) 431-2344
Guideposts Books & Inspirational Media Division
Designed by Cindy LaBreacht
Cover by Lookout Design Group
Typeset by Inside Out Design & Typesetting

Printed in the United States of America

Contents

Introduction vii

1 | Hometown Hilarity 1

2 | When the Porch Light Is On 29

3 | Dragging Main 47

4 | Over the Back Fence 67

5 | Front Pages and Front Porches 81

6 | Programs, Preachers, PTA, and Politics 105

7 | Neighborhood Nostalgia 133

8 | Outside the City Limits 163

Acknowledgments 193

Introduction

The sign outside the small town said, "Welcome to Grandview—home of 998 nice people . . . and one old grouch." The sign was right, of course, because it recognized the facts about towns and neighborhoods: most folks are pretty nice, but there's always one or two . . .

The truth is, no matter what size your town is or in what kind of neighborhood you find yourself, the experiences—both serious and funny—tend to repeat themselves.

Main Street Mirth will explore the sometimes funny, sometimes frustrating, sometimes friendly, sometimes kooky events and happenings in and around your town and neighborhood. And while the characters may bear different names, you'll probably find your fellow citizens and neighbors—and perhaps yourself—in these pages.

So kick off your shoes, and sit back for a few hours of good old hometown hilarity.

Let There Be Laughter! is a series of books created with one purpose in mind—to brighten your spirit, lighten your load, and give you delightful moments of restorative laughter. We at Guideposts assembled a team to look high and low for funny and wholesome writings that celebrate the lighter side of living. This series is the result of their research. And we hope you have as much fun reading it as they did putting it together.

You'll find stories relating hilarious, real-life tales; rib-tickling jokes and cartoons; absurd, frozen-moment-in-time anecdotes; top-ten lists and other miscellaneous grin-getters; great quotations that make you smile; and some of the best one-liners we've ever seen.

God gave us laughter! And believe it, He knew what He was doing. Because we wish you a dose of healthy fun and inspiration, we give you this book. In the midst of your everyday life, may it bring a smile to your face and true joy to your heart.

Let there be laughter!

The Editors

There ain't no use talking to God
when you ain't speakin' to your neighbor.

HAMBONE, *HAMBONE CARTOON STRIP*

1

Hometown Hilarity

What goes on around our town is a reflection of a town's personality, character . . . and, perhaps, characters. These town happenings are a constant source of hometown hilarity.

I DO—WITH LETTUCE, ONIONS, AND MUSTARD!

"Hey, Preacher, there's somebody out here on the sidewalk that wants to talk to you."

What followed was like a scene from an old western movie. Everything in Echols' Cafe came to a halt. Coffee cups were suspended in mid-air; Mrs. Echols, who was presiding over the cash register, rang up a bill and then forgot to take the money; and Johnny, the cook, stopped frying eggs and bacon and peeped through the small opening where prepared dishes were placed. All eyes focused for a moment on me and the table where I was having a second cup of coffee with some ranchers. Then as if in slow motion, the heads turned and the eyes focused through the windows on the strangers outside.

2 Main Street Mirth

I took a last sip of coffee, pushed my chair back, 'scused myself, and walked like a man toward whatever awaited me on Main Street, Walnut Springs, Texas—population 752 people and several thousand head of cattle. Most of my buddies set their cups down, picked up their hats, and followed me out the door. I knew, for I heard the shuffle of their chairs and the clomp of their boots.

Must be serious, I said to myself as I walked toward the strangers—a man and a woman. Anything's serious in Walnut Springs if it breaks up a good coffee-drinking session at Echols' Cafe on Saturday morning.

"Hi," I greeted them, "I'm the preacher." I never did like to be called *preacher*, but if they gave you a handle in this town, you lived with it.

The man said nothing; he just grinned at me. He was tall and lanky, and his hair was combed straight back and plastered down with some kind of heavy oil or cream. He was eating a hamburger. It was loaded with "the works"—meat, lettuce, onions, pickles, tomatoes, and mustard. Especially mustard. Between bites he would glance down proudly at the woman beside him.

She was much shorter than he in stature, had faded brown hair that was held down by bobby pins and clips, and wore a simple, drab print dress that came nearly to her ankles. Her hands were weathered from work, the kind of work done on a farm or ranch. Lines had begun to form on her face, but behind the lines was a hint of a nervous smile. It was obvious that she was shy and embarrassed.

"What can I do for you?" I asked as people gathered around us.

The man took another bite of his burger, chewed and savored it slowly, and said, "We want to get married, and we want to know if you'll do it."

With these words I gulped and looked down at the sidewalk. I couldn't afford to let this stranger see the fear in my eyes.

This was serious. He was asking me to marry them, and at this point as a seminary student I'd never performed a wedding ceremony. I'd only attended four weddings in my entire life. One of those was when I was four years old. Dad and I rode in his Model T Ford from Silver City, North Carolina, to Broadway where Aunt Beulah was getting married. I remember standing up and peeping over the dashboard most of the forty-mile journey, but I don't recall anything at all about the ceremony. Another wedding was my own, and I was too nervous to remember what the preacher said. I'd been to a couple of weddings of friends, but, frankly, I was more interested in decorating their cars than I was in observing the details of the service. I was a second-year seminary student, but marriage ceremonies had never been discussed in my classes.

I was in a mess—right here in the middle of Walnut Springs.

"Well," I replied with hesitation, "when would you like to get married?"

"Right now."

"Where?" I asked weakly.

"Right here's okay with us."

He grinned, took another bite of hamburger while she fidgeted awkwardly. The ranchers chuckled. They were really enjoying this.

I had to stall for time.

"I'll . . . I'll marry you," I said with as much confidence as I could muster, "but it will take a little while for me to get ready. And I don't think right here on the street is the best place. Why don't we meet at the Baptist Church around the corner in forty-five minutes."

She blushed shyly and said she liked the idea, for it would

give her a chance to go across the street to the variety store and purchase a new dress. He nodded his assent and I moved toward my old '41 Chevy that was parked at an angle in front of the cafe. Pausing before I opened the door, I swallowed hard, looked back at them and waved, hoping and praying that no one would guess the uncertainties churning inside me. She didn't see my wave for she was still looking shyly at the sidewalk.

But he looked me straight in the eyes and grinned broadly. I couldn't miss the grin for his mouth was outlined perfectly with mustard!

An older friend, Cecil Macbeth, was a seasoned pastor in Meridian, twelve miles east of Walnut Springs. When I reached the house I dialed him immediately and breathed a sigh of relief when he answered the phone.

"Cecil, I need help. Quick!"

"What's wrong, Bruce?"

"There's a couple over here in Walnut Springs that wants me to marry them."

"Well, go ahead and do it."

"I can't. I don't know how."

Cecil, a soft-spoken man, calmed me down and then asked if I had a copy of the *Pastor's Manual*.

"I think so," I replied hesitantly.

"Go find it and turn to the section on weddings. You'll find a sample of a ceremony on those pages. Just read that printed ceremony at the wedding and insert the names of the persons you're marrying."

"But I don't know their names," I protested.

"Well, my friend," he chuckled, "it's time you find out. And don't forget to sign the marriage license. Good luck."

Cecil also told me that we didn't need witnesses for weddings in Texas, so just the three of us showed up at the white frame church. I was relieved for I sure didn't want any of my coffee-drinking friends watching me stumble through this situation.

She was now wearing her new dress—a light blue clinging crepe one that came to her knees. It looked exactly like something that you would buy . . . well, it looked like something you would buy at a five-and-ten-cent store.

He was still wearing . . . mustard, clearly outlining his broad grin.

I closed the church doors, hoping and praying that no one would wander in.

They stood before me at the front of the little church and I read the introduction like an old pro. I had penciled their names in the black manual and breezed on through the "I dos." They did—without any hesitation.

We made it through the ring ceremony, after he had dug through his pockets searching for her wedding band. I led a prayer and then pronounced them "husband and wife."

She smiled shyly. He grinned again, leaned over, and kissed her.

When they turned to thank me, I also smiled . . . for the first time . . . for both their mouths were now clearly outlined with mustard.

I headed toward home, thankful for Cecil and the *Pastor's Manual*.

As I drove slowly down Main Street, Walnut Springs, I prayed out loud, "Please, dear God, I hope she likes . . . mustard."

Bruce McIver

SMALL-TOWN CAFÉ

The friendly small-town restaurant
Is busy as can be.
It serves as meeting place for all.
And town directory.

6 Main Street Mirth

Its grand aroma fills the air
With coffee, cakes, and pies
And gaily asks all young and old
To stop when passing by.

It stands for pop and ice-cream cones,
For chicken, golden brown,
For homespun hospitality,
The friendliest around.

Because it knows its clientele,
It's very apt to greet
A guest who has a birthday
With a very special treat.

It stands for warmth and cheerfulness
Where friends are surely found.
The cozy small-town restaurant
Lends pleasure to the town.

Craig E. Sathoff

JUST FOR POSTERITY

For $10, visitors to the country fair could ride in a barnstormer's biplane. An aging farm couple who'd never traveled outside the county thought they might like to take the opportunity to fly, just for posterity. But they were more than a little afraid.

"Tell you what," the barnstormer offered, perceiving their nervousness. "You can ride together, and I'll charge you only $5. Just promise me you won't scream or try to tell me how to fly my plane."

They accepted his offer and proceeded with the thrill of

their lives. Through a wild series of loops and rolls, the pilot never heard a sound from his backseat companions.

"Wow, Pop, you were just great!" shouted the pilot over his shoulder as he landed the plane. "I thought for sure you'd both holler when we made that nosedive."

"That wasn't so bad," yelled the farmer. "But I almost did break my promise a few minutes before that when my wife fell out of the airplane."

The Ultimate Joke Book

A small town is one where there is no place to go where you shouldn't.
Alexander Woollcott

You Know You Live in a Small Town When...

The "road hog" in front of you on Main Street is a farmer's combine.

Second Street is on the edge of town.

You leave your jacket on the back of the chair in the cafe, and when you go back the next day, it's still there, on the same chair.

You don't signal turns because everyone knows where you're going, anyway.

No social events can be scheduled when the school gym floor is being varnished.

Main Street Mirth

You call a wrong number and they supply you with the correct one.

Everyone knows all the news before it's published. They just read the hometown paper to see whether the publisher got it right.

The city limits signs are both on the same post!

The city jail is called Amoeba, because it only has one cell.

The McDonalds only has one Golden Arch.

The 7-11 is a 3 ½–5 ½.

The one-block-long Main Street dead-ends in both directions.

The phone book has only one page.

There's nothing doing every minute.

The ZIP code is a fraction.

Third Street is in the next town over.

A "night on the town" takes only 11 minutes.

The mayor had to annex property to eat a foot-long hot dog.

The New Year's baby was born in October.

Author Unknown

It was a small town, Ferguson, Ohio. When you entered there was a big sign and it said, "Welcome to Ferguson. Beware of the dog." The all-night drugstore closed at noon.

Jackie Vernon

Hometown Hilarity 9

"Remember son, when life hands you lemons, try, try again because a penny saved gathers no moss. That pretty much covers everything."

NOSTALGIA

At seven in the morning we reached Hannibal, Missouri, where my boyhood was spent . . . The only notion of the town that remained in my mind was the memory of it as I had known it when I first quitted it twenty-nine years ago. That picture of it was still as clear and vivid to me as a photograph.

I stepped ashore with the feeling of one who returns out of a dead-and-gone generation. . . . I passed through the vacant streets, still seeing the town as it was, and not as it is . . . and finally climbed Holiday's Hill to get a comprehensive view. The whole town lay spread out below me then, and I could mark and fix every locality, every detail.

The things about me and before me made me feel like a boy again—convinced me that I was a boy again, and that I had simply been dreaming an unusually long dream . . . From this vantage ground the extensive view up and down the river, and wide over the wooded expanses of Illinois, is very beautiful—one of the most beautiful on the Mississippi, it was satisfyingly beautiful to me . . . It had suffered no change; it was as young and fresh and comely and gracious as ever it had been; whereas, the faces of the others would be old, and scarred with the campaigns of life, and marked with their griefs and defeats, and would give me no upliftings of spirit.

During my three days' stay in the town, I woke up every morning with the impression that I was a boy—for in my dreams the faces were all young again, and looked as they had looked in the old times—but I went to bed a hundred years old, every night—for meantime I had been seeing those faces as they are now.

Mark Twain

THE OLD HOMETOWN

When it's near the close of day
   And months into years have grown,
There comes a feeling of delight
   As I think of the folks at home.
The old hometown has changed a lot,
   But one fact remains the same—
Through the years, no matter what,
   They never changed the name.

A creaking pump stands in the square,
   Not good as it used to be,
And there's yet a wooden bench
   Beneath the old elm tree.
Each year they hold a county fair,
   Its displays have gained renown,

And a weekly paper lets me know
What's happening in the old hometown.

I often think of an iron stove
Down at the village store
And how the menfolks, for a chat,
Would gather by the score.
When the hours are so lonely
And there's not a soul around,
It's then I think of all the folks
Back in the old hometown.

P. F. Freeman

THE PINSON MOUNDS

It was Friday night. I had been to Jackson, Tennessee, with my date and was now returning to the college we attended in Henderson. As we approached the thriving metropolis of Pinson—a city of seventy-five souls, known worldwide for the *Pinson Mounds* (nothing to do with candy bars)—the car started pulling radically to the left, which could only mean one thing—another flat tire. Incidentally, the Pinson Mounds are some rather nondescript small hills—heaps of earth—theoretically created by some aboriginal tribesmen during the sabre-toothed tiger era—with either burial, ceremonial, or religious connotations. I swerved quickly into a little roadside pullout sheltered by oak trees.

No, the pullout wasn't such a bad place, especially in view of who I was with, and I was never one to cast aside lightly what had obviously been made available to me providentially. But eventually, I knew I was going to have to do something. Joan was very understanding, but she had to be back in the dormitory by 10:30, or we would both have to stand trial before the D.C.—Discipline Committee—to explain our whereabouts on the night in question. I had already had the dubious honor, if not pleasure, of receiving a personal invitation to appear before this venerated and august group of sages on several previous occasions and had no desire for a return engagement.

Across the street from the pullout was a one-stall, combination repair shop, junk dealer, post office, hardware, gas station, you-name-it-we-got-it place. It had closed before dark, but the owner/proprietor's house was next door. It was my only hope. There were no lights on, and it was obvious that they were in bed. I knocked timidly at first, but getting no response and being rather desperate, I banged loudly. This aroused the dog, who, from the sound he made, must have resembled King Kong, but he was chained. I began to hear the angry mutterings and rumblings of someone who obviously had a deep resentment toward this unwarranted disruption of his nocturnal bliss.

A light went on, the door opened slightly, and then he appeared. His hair was disheveled, his pants, hastily thrown on over long-handled underwear—which also served as his nighttime attire—hung by one suspender. He was barefoot, his eyes were half-open, and when he opened the door, he had a most unpleasant expression on his face.

"Good evening sir," I said in my most cheerful, polite, and deferential tone.

"Good *morning* you mean," he said—neither cheerfully, politely, nor deferentially. "It's got to be after midnight—Whadayawant?"

"I'm very sorry to inconvenience you, sir, but you see, I have a problem."

"Don't give me that *inconvenience* rubbish—everybody's got problems, Sonny—even me," he said as he looked sourly and suspiciously at me.

"Oh really?" I said. "I'm sorry to hear that, but you see, I have a flat tire."

Hometown Hilarity 13

"Come back tomorrow." He started to close the door.

"But I can't do that," desperation was edging into my voice. "I'm from Freed-Hardeman, over in Henderson, and my girl has to be in the dorm by 10:30, and if I don't get her there, we'll be in big trouble." I tried to slide my foot forward so he couldn't close the door.

"Put your spare tire on."

"Well, sir, that's another problem. I don't *exactly* have a spare tire."

He emitted a long sigh of resignation and hopelessness, the kind of sigh that every parent learns all too quickly.

"Where's your car, Sonny?"

"Right over there behind those oaks," I said, as I pointed across the road.

"Okay. You go get the tire off and bring it over, and I'll fix it."

"Yes sir," I said enthusiastically. "But—well—actually, you see, I don't *exactly* have a jack either."

"Don't *exactly* have a jack? Son, either you have a jack or you don't have a jack. What *exactly* do you have? Do you have one *approximately*? Oh, forget it. There's one in that shed there beside the shop. Don't let Old Walt scare you; he's chained up. He sounds real fierce, but he's never *exactly* hurt anybody—seriously."

"Say, thanks a lot. You—uh—you wouldn't happen to have a lug wrench would you?"

"Oh, Lord, why me?" he muttered under his breath. "Yeah, there should be one in there with the jack," he said out loud. "Anything else you don't *exactly* have?"

"No sir," I said confidently, "that ought to just about do it."

It turned out that the jack was just about a foot from the end of Old Walt's chain, which looked very fragile. Old Walt was a bit much. He looked like a cross between a grizzly bear and a mountain lion, and he acted like he hadn't eaten in six weeks. He absolutely terrified me—lunging so hard against the end of his chain that he actually dragged his house, to which the chain was attached, behind him. His snarl began somewhere in the pit of his stomach, and by the time it came ripping, hissing, rattling, and roaring out his throat, it sounded like an avalanche. His eyes looked like laser beams, he had foam around his mouth, saliva dripped from his jaws, and when he snapped and ground his huge teeth, sparks flew. Old Walt was the original and archetypal *Junk Yard Dog*. I found a piece of rope, lassoed the jack, and dragged it close enough to me that I could grab it and run.

As I took the lug nuts off, I placed them in the hubcap for safe keeping. It was totally dark where the car was, and I had been too ashamed to ask for a flashlight, which I didn't *exactly* have either. The rim was rusted tightly to the drum, and I had to kick it with all my might to break it loose. When it finally flew off, it hit the edge of the hubcap and scattered the lug nuts in every direction, mostly under the car. I could only find one because the ground was about three inches deep in oak leaves. To make matters worse, I also discovered that I could see through my tire. It was absolutely ruined, and so was the inner tube. When I crossed the road again, tire in hand, I was simply wretched. My benefactor was in the garage.

"I don't think this tire is any good," I said apologetically. "You don't *happen* to have one do you?"

"I don't *happen* to have nothin', Sonny. What I got here I got *on purpose*, and I do have one." He rummaged around and eventually found a pretty decent tire.

"I could let you have this one for five bucks."

"Do you have one any less expensive? I don't *exactly* have five dollars," I said.

"How *much* less expensive? Maybe I could let it go for three," he said.

"I don't *exactly* have three either."

"Well, how much *exactly* do you have?" he said with exasperation.

"Well, if you put it in *exact* terms," I reached in my front pocket and counted out the change, "I have thirty-five cents," I said hopefully.

At that very moment, Joan appeared. She had grown tired of waiting and had come to see if I was making any progress.

Joan was very, very pretty.

"Who in the world is this?" he said, with a whistle and obvious admiration in his voice.

"Oh, this is Joan; she's my date."

He looked appreciatively at Joan.

"You sure must be some *talker,* Sonny. She sure didn't go with you for your *looks,* your *money,* your *brains,* or your *car.*"

A pretty girl does wonders to men. His whole attitude changed in Joan's presence. He became gracious, kind, even cheerful—he forgot his inconvenience. He *gave* me the tire, found a tube, patched it, found some spare lug nuts, and helped me put it on. He even invited me to stop by and visit with him on my next trip to Jackson—if I brought Joan.

He smiled when I told him I would try to repay him someday. "Oh," he said, "that's okay. Forget it. I'll get more than my money's worth telling this story over the next twenty-five years. But nobody will believe it."

John William Smith

•••

We went out at 10 p.m., did the town, and went home at 10:15.

Rusty Wright and Linda Raney Wright

•••

MYSTERY

A fellow was raised in the back hills of West Virginia—I mean, so far out in the sticks, never in his life had he seen a big city, to say nothing of modern inventions and neon lights. He married a girl just like himself and they spent all their married years in the backwoods. They had one son, whom they creatively named Junior. Around the time Junior reached his sixteenth birthday, his dad began to realize it wouldn't be too many years before their son would become a man and would strike out on his own. It troubled him that his boy could reach manhood and wind up getting a job in the city, not prepared to face the real world. He felt responsible and decided to do something about it.

He and his wife started saving for a trip the three of them would take to the city. About three years later the big day arrived. They tossed their belongings in the ol' pickup and started the long journey over winding, rough roads to the city. Their plan was to spend several days at a swanky hotel and take in all the sights. As they approached the outskirts of the metropolis, Papa began to get a little jumpy: "Mama, when we pull up at th' hotel, you stay in th' truck while Junior an' I go in an' look around. We'll come back and git ya, OK?" She agreed.

Flashing neon lights and uniformed doormen greeted them as they pulled up. Mama stayed put as Papa and Junior walked wide-eyed into the lobby. Neither could believe his eyes! When they stepped on a mat, the doors opened automatically. Inside, they stood like statues, staring at the first chandelier either of them had ever seen. It hung from a ceiling three stories high. Off to the left was an enormous waterfall, rippling over inlaid stones and rocks. "Junior, look!" Papa was pointing toward a long mall where busy shoppers were going in and out of beautiful stores. "Papa, looka there!" Down below was an ice-skating rink—*inside*.

While both stood silent, watching one breathtaking sight after another, they kept hearing a clicking sound behind them. Finally, Papa turned around and saw this amazing little room with doors that slid open from the center. "What in the world?" People would walk up, push a button and wait. Lights would flicker above the doors and then, "click," the doors would slide open from the middle. Some people would walk out of the little room and others would walk inside and turn around as, "click," the doors slid shut. By now, dad and son stood *totally* transfixed.

At that moment a wrinkled old lady shuffled up to the doors all by herself. She pushed the button and waited only a few seconds. "Click," the doors opened with a swish and she hobbled into the little room. No one else stepped in with her, so "click," the doors slid shut. Not more than twenty seconds later the doors opened again—and there stood this fabulously attractive blond, a young woman in her twenties—high heels, shapely body, beautiful face—a real knockout! As she stepped out, smiled, and turned to walk away, Papa nudged his boy and mumbled, "Hey, Junior . . . *go git Mama!*"

Michael Green

A community is like a ship, everyone ought to be prepared to take the helm.

Henrik Ibsen

You Might Be City Folk If . . .

You don't have any problems pronouncing "Worcestershire sauce" correctly.

For breakfast, you would prefer potatoes au gratin to grits.

You don't know what a Moon Pie is.

You've never, ever, eaten okra.

You eat fried chicken with a knife and fork.

You have no idea what a polecat is.

You don't see anything wrong with putting a sweater on a poodle.

You would rather have your son become a lawyer than grow up to get his own TV fishing show.

You've never planned your summer vacation around a gun and knife show.

You think more money should go to important scientific research at your university than to the salary of the head football coach.

You don't have at least one can of WD-40 somewhere around the house.

The last time you smiled was when you beat someone to an on-ramp on the freeway.

You don't have any hats in your closet that advertise feed stores.

You can't spit out the car window without pulling over to the side of the road and stopping.

Becky Freeman

BANK

A man in Wichita, Kansas, received a computerized bill for nothing. The balance due column read $0.00. He threw it away.

A month later the same store sent another bill with the following notation: "This account is now past due." He circled the zeros and sent the bill back to the store.

A few days later he received another scorching computerized letter. It admonished him to pay his debt of $0.00. Realizing that nothing can be quite as stubborn as a computer, he finally sat down and wrote out a check for $0.00. He received no further pleas from the store.

Tal D. Bonham

•••

Milkman: Are you sure you want 54 quarts of milk?
Lady: Yes. My doctor told me to take a bath in milk.
Milkman: Do you want it pasteurized?
Lady: No, just up to my chin.

Bob Phillips

•••

A CONVERSATION WITH ROYALTY

I am looking for a prince in our hometown. He must be chivalrous, handsome, able to save damsels in distress, and generous to his in-laws. This search stems from a postbirthday conversation with my six-year-old daughter.

A golden opportunity for discovery presented itself when we were in the car with the radio blaring. I turned off the background noise and engaged her.

"Shannon," I asked, "what do you want to be when you grow up? What do you—"

"A princess," she interrupted.

"No, I mean what do you want to *do* when you grow up?"

"I want to be a nurse," she said matter-of-factly.

Her second answer was much more practical. But I could tell her heart was really in the first response.

"Didn't you say you wanted to be a princess first?"

"Yeah."

"Why do you want to be a princess?"

She told me all the things princesses get to wear. Frilly things. Jewelry that costs a lot of money. Princesses also get to ride around in carriages and wave at the little people. Princesses have tea whenever they want and have maids and butlers waiting on them at all hours. Princesses sleep in a soft bed with a canopy overhead. It sounded so good I thought about becoming one myself.

"How do you think you'll get to become a princess?"

She sighed heavily and said, "I guess I'd have to marry a prince."

"Mmmm," I said. "And where do you think you'll find one of those?"

She thought a moment before turning her blue eyes toward me. "Are there any in Bolingbrook?"

Bolingbrook is the hamlet we call home. I haven't seen any castles here, other than the big white one that sells cheese-burgers. I bit my lip and turned to the broken lines of I-35—anything to keep from smiling. She was still looking at me when I turned and said, "I don't know of any, but then I don't know everyone in Bolingbrook."

"They have them in England," she said. "They get to live in castles and things."

"True. But if you moved to England, you wouldn't be able to see your sisters or brothers. You would be an awfully long way from Mom and Dad, too."

"That's okay," she said. 'You guys can come with me."

We ran our errands and stopped by a bookstore. Then we were off to a special restaurant for lunch. Princesses can really put away the chicken fingers and french fries.

We talked about her party the day before. We talked about her friends and her school and her new doll. We talked about the ketchup. We talked about the toll booth and where the money goes when you throw it in. We talked about dessert.

These are things on a princess's mind, so we talked about all of them and kept the radio off.

"Do you want to get married?" I asked.

"Not really," she said. "But I guess I do, because I want to have babies."

The makeup was still faint from her party; blue eye shadow was caked below her brow, a splash of rouge on her cheeks. There were even a few sparkles left from the glittery fingernail polish. Her blond hair was drawn back tightly in a ponytail. She giggled and I could see all those wonderful baby teeth.

You don't have to marry a prince to be a princess, I thought.

Chris Fabry

BACK-HOME THOUGHTS

What is wrong with too many of us is we never get to spend any time in places like Palatka, Florida, anymore.

I'm not saying I'm ready to pack it up and move to Palatka right now, but I spent a couple of days there recently, and I'm better off for it.

Palatka has a population of about twelve thousand. It sits on the banks of the St. Johns River, wide and blue, sixty miles south of Jacksonville.

There's a paper mill and a furniture factory.

I made a speech in a place that is a country and western juke joint on the weekends.

"Not much to do in Palatka," a man apologized to me.

I wouldn't say that. Country star John Conlee was due in the juke joint soon, and Palatka calls itself the bass-fishing capital of the world.

Unless you've been to a country juke joint on a Saturday night or bass-fished with somebody who knows where the glory holes are, your life is miserably incomplete.

There's a Holiday Inn in Palatka. It has one of those satellite dishes that enables first-run movies to be shown in the rooms for a price. I stayed in the Holiday Inn and ordered a Nick Nolte movie called *Weeds*. Next to *Kiss of the Spider Woman*, it was the worst movie I'd ever seen.

But that's the only bad thing that happened to me in Palatka.

My first morning, I went to the Holiday Inn restaurant and ordered my eggs the same way I always order them: "over medium well."

That means the yellow doesn't run out of the egg, it merely *crawls*.

Rarely do I ever get my eggs cooked correctly. In Palatka I did. Plus, when the waitress served my eggs, she smiled and said, "If these aren't cooked the way you like them, just tell me and I'll get 'em done over for you."

There is a place in heaven for smiling, cooperative waitresses.

I played golf in Palatka at the municipal course, the only one in town. It was packed.

"It's the Yankees," a local explained to me. "They come down this time of year. We get the poor ones. The rich ones go on down to Ft. Lauderdale or Palm Beach."

The course was charming. So was my partner, who at one point in the match made five straight birdies.

"They take golf real seriously in Palatka," the pro was saying.

Perhaps it was the sunshine that got to me. It was the first time I'd had off from winter for a while.

Or maybe it was the people I met. There was a warmth to them, too. Throw in the eggs and the smiling waitress and how gorgeous the river looked in the morning, and I started getting all those back-home thoughts again.

So many of us sprang from origins like Palatka, only to be gobbled by the urban monster.

But you can go back. And I will someday. To my Palatka.

I'm not certain where that is just yet, but the thing is, I've started looking. For that, I thank Palatka.

Lewis Grizzard

© Dan Piraro. Reprinted with permission of King Features syndicate.

THE LEMONADE STAND

Along with Scripture verses, choruses, manners and the proper dress code, the greatest thing my mother passed on to us was the gift of adaptation. I am almost certain that my mother invented the phrase "When life gives you lemons..." Mom and Dad instilled in us not only the joy of a good glass of lemonade but also the thrill of making it yourself.

We never considered ourselves well-off financially. We seldom considered ourselves poor. We simply didn't consider *ourselves*. My wardrobe was filled with hand-me-downs and homemade dresses my grandmother would send us every fall for the upcoming school year. When we wore shoes, they were usually tennis shoes or sandals. Since we lived in the South, barefoot was vogue!

There did come a brief time when the realization that "We *are* poor" hit us all. Mother couldn't find a job. Dad had just accepted a call to a small church in Orangeburg, South Carolina. Mike had gone to a college 500 miles away, and Charlotta was soon to follow. I can remember hearing Mom and Dad argue about the possibility of getting food stamps. I don't think it was as much a matter of pride as it was that Mom still didn't consider us desperate enough. She would say, "But what if someone else needs them more?"

As I sat at the dinner table eating for the fifth time that week a sandwich made with government cheese and grilled with government butter, I looked at her and said, "Mom, who could need 'em worse than us?"

So one afternoon Mom and I stood in the food stamp line for more than three hours. Of course, after we got them, the whole family wanted in on the selection process at the grocery store. Grocery shopping had never been so exciting. Everyone was thrilled to pick out the food, but as soon as we approached the checkout counter, they all scrambled to the car—except for Mom and me. When Mother handed the girl at the Piggly Wiggly our little booklet, I grinned at Mother and said in my most Southern-belle, Scarlet O'Hara voice, "I'll tell the driver to bring the limo around, Mother, and pick us up at the door. I know how you hate to wait in this summer heat." When the food stamps ran out, we went back to grilled cheese until things began to pick up at the church again.

Mother had toyed a long time with the idea of going to nursing school. When she heard that Baptist Hospital in Columbia, South Carolina, was offering a two-year Licensed Practical Nurse (LPN) course, she decided that this would be the year. She and Dad argued about her decision for hours—but for some reason, Mother truly felt nursing school was something she was called to do. She borrowed the money from her mother, and at the age of 40 off to school she went.

She drove 91 miles round trip to nursing school every day. Cheralyn and I made flash cards and quizzed her for exams. She amazed us all. Mother had not been in school in 22 years and would have failed chemistry in high school twice had it not been for the tutor her mom and dad had hired during her senior year. She passed nursing school with flying colors, and we proudly attended her graduation from LPN school. (Dad had refused to attend—but near the end of the ceremony we noticed him on the back row of that huge auditorium in Columbia.)

While Mom was in nursing school, Cheralyn and I had almost full responsibility of the house. We had our regular chores to do as well as cooking most of the meals. We were proud of our diverse menus: macaroni and cheese, peanut butter and jelly, Froot Loops—and on special occasions (or Friday, whichever came first) *hot dogs!*

Did I mention that we lived on a tight budget? We had a few poundings from the church folks—but you get mostly dusty, dented cans of yams and cranberry sauce at those things! So Cheralyn and I decided the answer to our menu problem was simply to grow our own garden. We worked for hours getting the soil ready. We saved our money and went down to the local hardware store and purchased seed packets of green beans, corn, cucumbers, and tomatoes. The weeds outgrew our patience, and our sandy Southern soil could produce nothing—nothing but cucumbers, that is.

They were everywhere! We had a long vine of cucumbers that stretched from the front porch of our house, across the church parking lot, and up the steps of the fellowship hall. We made cucumber sandwiches, cucumber salad, fried cucumbers—anything you could make with cucumbers, we made. Some things you couldn't make with cucumbers we made anyway. And we ate them all.

Then just like the plagues finally ended in Egypt, we received a sweet reprieve from our cucumber suppers. A man in our church raised hogs for his chain of barbecue restaurants. He called the house one evening to say that the next morning he would be stopping by with a package for the pastor and his family. Hallelujah!

Cheralyn and I rewrote our menu for the next month: barbecued pork chops, ribs, ham, bacon—we even made plans for the ears and the feet. We set the table that night for tomorrow's dinner. We were so excited we could hardly sleep. (Or maybe it was the cucumbers!)

Nevertheless, as promised, an old pickup truck pulled into the driveway the next afternoon. A kind old farmer climbed out of his truck carrying a huge package wrapped in brown paper. The front of his apron was bloody, but we hardly pitied the beast we would dine on for the next few weeks. We could smell something spicy and delicious as he set the package on the counter. We had envisioned a huge country ham, perhaps a pork roast, maybe slabs of bacon. We couldn't wait for him to leave so we could dive in.

Mother thanked him very kindly, and as the front door clicked shut, Cheralyn and I ripped open our mouth-watering feast. There it was—a fresh, meaty, 15-pound roll of *bologna!* Now don't get me wrong. I don't dislike bologna. But a couple of skinny little preacher's kids had waited all day long for pork chops and had gotten bologna—disappointing bologna.

When mother fixed supper that night, we were surprised to see something shaped like pork chops on our plates. Mother had used some of her arts and crafts skills to cut little pork chop shapes out of the bologna and fried it until it was crisp. Served with cold, sliced cucumbers and cornbread, Mom showed us how to make lemonade out of lemons.

The next day the doorbell rang. A young lady stood on our porch and explained to Mother how she had noticed the church next door and wondered if we knew how to reach the pastor. Mother invited her in. With watery eyes, she told Mother that her children were hungry and that her husband had been out of work for several months. Her food stamps had run out too. Without question, Mom quickly filled a grocery sack with cucumbers and cut our much-needed roll of bologna in half and shared it with this stranger. They shared a glass of lemonade before she left, and we never saw her again.

Chonda Pierce

•••

Small Town: Where people go to church on Sunday to see people who didn't.
Lowell D. Streiker

•••

It was such a small town we didn't even have a village idiot. We had to take turns.

Billy Holliday

2

When the Porch Light Is On

Small towns and communities each have their own unique signs and signals of what's happening in town. Sometimes these signs and signals prompt funny stories and moments of nostalgia.

THE PORCH LIGHT'S ON. WHO DIED?

Grandview, Texas. The sign read, "Population 984 wonderful people and one old grouch." We had one 4-way blinking red light where the highway crossed our main street. We didn't really *need* a light there, we just wanted to make sure people whizzing through on the two-lane highway at least slowed up enough to see that there *was* a town.

It was almost a mile from one end of town to the other. One good blink and you missed it. On Saturday night—and most every other night—teenagers "drug" the strip in beat-up convertibles and revved-up, stripped-down jalopies. In our black high school letter jackets with gold leather sleeves, and with the rock 'n' roll station blaring, man, were we hot!

We had twenty-one students in my graduating class. Of that twenty-one there were seven couples who married each other. And I alone escaped to tell about it.

The way you knew somebody in town had died was that the funeral home (which was also the funeral director's house) left the front porch light on. Since it was right across the street from the post office, where you had to go pick up your mail (no local delivery), you couldn't miss it. Sounds quaint, and maybe it was, but it worked. Soon the phone lines were buzzing, and before long everybody knew who was laid out for viewing.

> **The nice thing about a small town is that when you don't know what you're doing, someone else always does.**

The nice thing about a small town is that when you don't know what you're doing, someone else always does. Between my junior and senior years in high school, I spent the summer working at a Christian youth camp in East Texas called Camp Deer Run—about three hours away. I was gone about ten weeks—from early June to mid-August.

When camp was over, my parents were coming to get me. Since the camp was not too far from my grandparents' home, they decided to let the trip do double duty. So my dad—preacher at one of the local churches—borrowed a pickup from one of the church deacons and loaded a mattress and box springs in the back. Then he and my mom drove to East Texas, dropped off the bedding at my grandparents', and picked me up at camp. We arrived back home in Grandview on Friday evening.

On Saturday I walked the three blocks from our house to downtown Grandview, which consisted primarily of a small variety store, a drugstore (with an old fashioned soda fountain), a bank, a newspaper, and a grocery store. As I was walking toward the drugstore, I met a woman I knew, who said, "Well, Mary! What are *you* doing here?"

Thinking she meant that she was surprised to see me home from camp, I said, "Well, I've been away at camp all summer and just got home last night."

With a puzzled look she replied, "No. What I mean is, I heard that your mother and daddy just packed up all their belongings and moved out of town without telling anyone."

I laughed. "You're kidding, right?"

"No, really. Someone saw them driving out of town with a pickup full of furniture."

Welcome to a small town.

But there are advantages to living in a small town too. As the old *Cheers* TV show theme song said, it's "where everybody knows your name." And there's comfort in that.

For instance, I had an old '49 Ford that I bought for fifty dollars just before my senior year. It was a two-toned car—navy blue and rust. In a couple of places the rust color had eaten almost all the way through the metal. The seat covers were orange floral, because I'd used an old bedspread to cover up the holes in the original ones that were worn out. If I got old Jingles over 45 mph, she shook like she had the palsy. And I wasn't allowed to go out of town in her at all for fear she wouldn't make it there or back.

When Jingles ran out of gas about once a week because the gas gauge didn't work, I could just call Stu down at the gas station, and he'd bring me some gas. Then I could pay him the end of the week when I got my check from the "dime store" where I worked for fifty cents an hour. He trusted me because, after all, I was the preacher's kid. Besides, he knew where I lived.

Stu would say, "Mary, when are you gonna git this thing fixed?"

And I'd say, "I can't afford it, Stu; you know that. It would cost more to fix the gas gauge than I paid for the whole car."

"Oh, yeah. Well, okay. Just call me then." And the next week I would.

Another benefit to being in a small town was lunch. When I was a junior, I ran around with another junior and two seniors. We ate lunch together every day. On Monday we went to Marsha's house for tuna and mushroom soup on toast. On Tuesday we went to Cheryl's house, and her mom cooked lunch for us. On Wednesday we ate at the local restaurant. On Thursday we ate at my house, and my mom fixed lunch. And on Friday we went to Janie's for ham-and-cheese sandwiches, Ruffles, and Cokes.

We especially liked Wednesdays. We would call Jennie at the restaurant about 11:00 and order our lunch. She'd have it sitting on the table waiting for us when we walked in at 12:10. It was one of our favorite rituals. You just can't do that in a big city.

My senior year I worked at the post office. My friend N. F. Hale was the acting postmaster, and when the government announced a special "student program" for the post office, he asked me if I wanted the job. Of course, I jumped at the chance. And I was walking in tall cotton! While most of my friends were making about $0.90 an hour, I was making $3.50 an hour. Whew! It made my head spin.

I had to be at work every morning at six. So, I got up at five, dressed quietly so as not to wake up my folks, and drove to the cafe for breakfast. My friend and classmate Cody ran a milk route, so he was always there too. And another one of our friends nicknamed Bokie waited tables. Most everyone else in the restaurant at that hour was an old farmer or school bus driver.

Cody and I liked to play the jukebox at breakfast. So we faithfully fed it nickels to hear our favorite 1960s tunes.

Somehow the old farmers didn't appreciate having to drink their coffee and read their papers with the Rollin' Stones grinding out "I can't get no satisfaction" at 5:30 A.M. Of course, we thought it was funny.

We also liked to play tricks on Bokie. So instead of a real tip, we'd leave her some S&H Green Stamps. Or we'd drop her tip into a glass of water so she had to fish it out. Nothing really destructive; just for fun. But if you did that today in a big city restaurant, you'd probably end up in jail.

I really love small towns. They're special. They have character. In fact, some of them have several real characters. I miss my small town.

Ahh, sweet memories of days gone by. . . .

Mary Hollingsworth

DOC BRACKETT

Doc Brackett didn't have black whiskers.

Nonetheless, he was a fine man.

He doctored in Our Town for many years. He doctored more people than any other doctor in Our Town but made less money.

That was because Doc Brackett was always doctoring poor people, who had no money to pay.

He would get up in the middle of the coldest night and ride twenty miles to doctor a sick woman, or child, or to patch up some fellow who got hurt.

Everybody in Our Town knew Doc Brackett's office over Rice's clothing store. It was up a narrow flight of stairs. His office was always filled with people. A sign at the foot of the stairs said: DR. BRACKETT, OFFICE UPSTAIRS.

Doc Brackett was a bachelor. He was once supposed to marry Miss Elvira Cromwell, the daughter of old Junius Cromwell, the banker, but on the day the wedding was supposed to take place Doc Brackett got a call to go out into the country and doctor a Mexican child.

Miss Elvira got sore at him and called off the wedding. She said that a man who would think more of a Mexican child than of his wedding was no good. Many women in Our Town agreed with Miss Elvira Cromwell, but the parents of the Mexican child were very grateful to Doc Brackett when the child recovered.

For forty years, the lame, and the halt, and the blind of Our Town had climbed up and down the stairs to Doc Brackett's office.

He never turned anybody away.

But he lived to be seventy years old, and then one day he keeled over on the sofa in his office and died. By this time his black hair had turned white.

Doc Brackett had one of the biggest funerals ever seen in Our Town. Everybody went to pay their last respects when he was laid out in Gruber's undertaking parlors. He was buried in Riverview Cemetery.

There was talk of raising money to put a nice tombstone on Doc Brackett's grave as a memorial. The talk got as far as arguing about what should be carved on the stone about him. Some thought poetry would be very nice.

Doc Brackett hated poetry.

The matter dragged along and nothing whatever was done.

Then one day George Gruber, the undertaker, said that Doc Brackett's memorial was already over his grave, with an epitaph and all. George Gruber said the Mexican parents of the child Doc Brackett saved years ago had worried about him having no tombstone.

They had no money themselves, so they took the sign from the foot of the stairs at Doc Brackett's office and stuck it over his grave: It read: DR. BRACKETT, OFFICE UPSTAIRS.

Damon Runyon

FUNERAL HOME FANS AND TONGUE DEPRESSORS

I grew up attending a little Swedish Methodist Church in the country. During the services, I'd sit in the back pew with my buddies and have a good time. We tried to pay attention, but sometimes it was hard. Even though we had a great preacher, my heart just wasn't always into the sermon. Sometimes I took a bulletin and filled in the *O*s and the *B*s and the *D*s. (Tell the truth and shame the devil—you've done it too!)

We didn't always have bulletins, though, in that little church outside of Austin. But we always had funeral-home fans. Thank God for the funeral home that provided us with those fans. We'd just fan ourselves like crazy, and that would give us something to do. On one side of the fan was a picture of Jesus praying on a rock or knocking on a door. On the other side was the funeral home's advertisement displaying different kinds of caskets, types of metal, and things like that. A local doctor had donated some tongue depressors for us to staple onto the fans so they'd have handles.

I can remember taking a tongue depressor stapled to a fan and using it to "examine" an unwitting friend. The man behind us scolded, "Dennis, get that thing off his tongue right now. No telling how many other people have had it on their tongues." Of course, back then I didn't worry about germs or diseases like we do nowadays.

As I recall, we Methodists just used one staple in our tongue depressors because we were methodical and steady right down the line. My Baptist buddies usually used two staples to keep their fans attached, because they got sort of excited during their occasional week-long revivals. And if a lady in the Baptist choir ever got upset about not being picked to sing a solo, it sort of helped to have two staples in her fan. My Pentecostal and charismatic friends usually needed three staples in their tongue depressors because they always got excited, and they tended to throw their fans across the room in moments of joy.

Dennis Swanberg

••

Six prominent men were named as pallbearers in the will of a man who had died penniless, owing each of them considerable sums.

"They have been wonderful creditors," the will said, "and I would like to have them carry me to the end."

Tal D. Bonham

••

YOU MIGHT BE IN A COUNTRY CHURCH IF...

...FINDING AND RETURNING LOST SHEEP
IS NOT JUST A PARABLE.

David Espurvoa © Ron Birk

In a cemetery:
> Persons are prohibited from picking flowers from any but their own graves.
> *Lowell D. Streiker*

ALL IT TAKES IS A LITTLE MOTIVATION

A gentleman worked on the 4:00 P.M. to midnight shift, and he always walked home after work. One night the moon was shining so bright he decided to take a shortcut through the cemetery, which would save him roughly a half-mile walk. There were no incidents involved, so he repeated the process on a regular basis, always following the same path. One night as he was walking his route through the cemetery, he did not realize that during the day a grave had been dug in the very center of his path. He stepped right into the grave and immediately started desperately trying to get out. His best efforts failed him, and after a few minutes, he decided to relax and wait until morning when someone would help him out.

He sat down in the corner and was half asleep when a drunk stumbled into the grave. His arrival roused the shift worker since the drunk was desperately trying to climb out, clawing frantically at the sides. Our hero reached out his hand, touched the drunk on the leg, and said, "Friend, you can't get out of here . . . "—but he did! Now that's motivation.
Zig Ziglar

Did you hear about the undertaker who closes all his letters with "Eventually yours"?

Bob Phillips

MY GRAVE CONCERN

When Mom comes to visit, the first place she wants to go is the graveyard. It's usually an all-day affair. My family has almost as many skeletons below ground as in the closet.

"Oh, there's your great-uncle Harvey," Mom says, pulling Sis and me to a stop in front of a tilting tombstone. "You remember Uncle Harvey."

Uncle Harvey used to find great joy in putting his glass eye in the coleslaw at family reunions. No amount of therapy could get me to eat coleslaw now.

Mom, never having seen much distinction between the living and the dead, is dressed like she's having tea with the queen. My little sister is going through her "Madonna meets the Cherokee" phase. And I'm in my usual "fashion follows function." If I had on a hard hat, we'd look like a female version of the Village People.

Even if Mom owned a pair of sensible shoes, I doubt she'd wear them. On this particular day she's teetering on two-inch red spikes. Every time she takes a step, her heels drive into the ground like tent stakes. Then, with the momentum of pulling her foot free, her knee pops up to her waist. She looks like a cross between a Rockette and a Tennessee walking horse.

With Sis at one elbow and me at the other, Mom aerates the memorial lawn.

"Dear Aunt Molly," Mom says. "The finest teacher in the county."

Dear Aunt Molly used to entertain us by dressing up in a

grass skirt and bra, and doing the hula while reciting risqué limericks.

When we get to an unusually well-kept grave, Mom seems to draw a blank.

"Oh, cousin Claudia," she finally says, reading the marker. It doesn't ring a bell for me. I look over at Sis. She's yawning.

"Oh, you remember, Claudia," Mom says. "She was a very good housekeeper."

Well, that narrows it down.

Other than her victory over dust, Claudia must have been as boring as toast. Mom pulls out a compact and checks her teeth for lipstick. Sis lights a cigarette, and I chew off a hangnail. After a respectable amount of time, we move on.

Apparently, this party isn't moving fast enough to suit Mom. Pulling free, she wobbles on tiptoe while Sis and I lean against a tree to enjoy the ambiance.

Our family graveyard is what a graveyard should be, old and spooky.

Nowadays, they plant you like corn, in perfectly straight rows with perfectly uniform markers flat on the ground, so they don't have to weed-eat. I would die. I want my eternal resting place to be wild and unpredictable, with my headstone just slightly off center and facing in whatever direction I choose. In other words, I want death to resemble life as much as possible.

Our family graveyard is what a graveyard should be, old and spooky.

To end up like cousin Claudia makes me shudder. When my relatives stand in front of my grave, I want them to have something to talk about.

"If I turn into a boring person," I say, "I want you to let me know."

Slowly, Sis exhales a chain of white rings into my face.

"Consider yourself notified," she says.

It is a brief moment of sisterly love. Mom has mired at Great Aunt Hattie's and we have to go dig her out.

P. S. Wall

It is not always easy to say the right thing on the spur of the moment. We can sympathize with the chap who met an old friend after many years.

"How is your wife?"

"She is in heaven," replied the friend.

"Oh, I'm sorry," stammered the chap. Then he realized this was not the thing to say. "I mean," he stammered, "I'm glad." That seemed even worse so he blurted, "Well, what I really mean is, I'm surprised."

Bob Phillips

SIGNS OF THE TIMES

We have taller buildings but shorter tempers.
Wilder motorways but narrower viewpoints.
We spend more, but we have less.
We buy more, but enjoy it less.
We have bigger houses and smaller families.
More conveniences, but less time.
We have more degrees, but less common sense.
More knowledge, but less judgment.
More experts, but more problems.
More medicine, but less well being.
We have multiplied our possessions, but reduced our values.
We talk too much, but lie too often.

When the Porch Light Is On

We've learned how to make a living, but not how to live life.
We have added years to life, but not life to years.
We've been all the way to the moon and back, but can't cross the street to help a neighbor.
We write more, but learn less.
We plan more, but accomplish less.
We have higher incomes but lower morals.
We have more acquaintances but fewer friends.

These are times of fast foods and slow digestion.
Tall men and short character.
Steep profits and shallow relationships.

These are times of world peace but domestic warfare.
More leisure and less fun.
More kinds of food, but less nutrition.

These are days of two incomes, but more divorce.
Of fancier houses but broken homes.

It is a time when there is much in the shop window
And nothing in the stock room.

J. John and Mark Stibbe

••

I'm originally from the Ozarks. Not everyone in the Ozarks lives in a trailer park. There's a huge waiting list.

Nancy Norton

••

SHE "DADE"

My dad worked for the funeral director, and his daughters were my best friends. I remember one time their doorbell rang—they lived in one side of this big house with a wraparound porch, and the funeral home was in the other side. Clayton Kay—the dad and funeral director—went to the door, and a hispanic man was standing there with a dead woman in his arms.

Clayton said, "Here now, what's wrong with her?"

He said simply, "She dade."

"Well, you can't just bring her in here like this. You have to have a doctor pronounce her dead at the hospital. Then we'll pick her up there."

"She DADE," he said simply as he pushed into the parlor past Clayton and laid the woman on the sofa.

"Now, listen, sir," said Clayton sternly, "you *cannot* just leave her here like this."

"She DADE," he repeated clearly and walked out the door, leaving Clayton to figure out what to do.

We laughed about that one for weeks. I love small towns—they're a riot.

Mary Hollingsworth

THE WAY TO GO

An old preacher was dying. He requested that his IRS agent and his lawyer come to his home. When they entered his bedroom, the preacher motioned for them to sit on each side of the bed.

Both the IRS agent and lawyer were touched that the old preacher wanted to be with them during his final moments. They were also curious, because the preacher had never particularly liked either one of them. Finally, the lawyer asked, "Pastor, why did you ask us to come?"

The old preacher mustered up some strength, then said weakly, "Jesus died between two thieves, and that's how I want to go too."

Jim K. Raus

A VISIT TO THE CEMETERY

Mother called, wanting me to take part in her little ritual: a visit to the cemetery. It is a ritual I'm not sure I understand, but it is important to Mother, so I go. It's not at all that I mind spending a few dollars for flowers. And I don't mind the drive there or the amount of time it takes for this ritual. And I certainly don't mind a visit or two on special occasions. Placing flowers at Charlotta and Cheralyn's graves is one thing, but having a picnic complete with fried chicken and potato salad—well, that's just a bit much for me. It seems that passing the KFC bucket around is a real reminder that they are not here, sitting in our circle. It is a reminder that they are gone—there in the ground. Dead. Cold. Gone. I don't like those reminders. I like placing flowers in their favorite colors in the church, commemorating their birthdays and their favorite seasons. Those are living memorials, and I like that best. I'm just weird, I guess!

Despite my own preferences on the matter, when Mother calls and wants to make that drive (picnic) to Forest Hill, I try to make sure she doesn't go alone. At this particular time in Mother's life—physically struggling through chemotherapy— I wasn't sure it was a good idea to hang out in the cemetery. It's hard enough to go to those two heart-shaped granite slabs with your last name printed across the front, but to go when you are facing an uphill battle with cancer—that's just not a real encouraging place to hang out.

I tried my best to suggest another day, but for some reason or other she needed to go today. "You know, Mom, we'll have better weather tomorrow."

"I know," she said, "but I've already made the potato salad for the grandkids." What could I say!

I picked up Mom and then we stopped for my two nephews, Josh (then age 15) and Jacob (age 10), who piled into the van with my kids, and we all headed to the cemetery. We made our normal stop at the little market in town that sold small potted plants and bought some red geraniums and some cut daisies, then on to KFC for original recipe (all white meat), and finally headed to the top of the hill where Cheralyn and Charlotta are buried.

After a difficult month of chemotherapy, Mother had lost all of her hair and her immune system was quite compromised, so we made her agree not to stay in the wind for too long. We climbed out of the van and made our way across the grounds, stopping once in awhile to take a look at the names of new markers draped with fresh-cut flowers left from recent funeral services.

As we made our way through the garden of granite statues, a gust of wind whipped up, taking with it a few of our newly purchased daisies—and Mother's newly purchased hair! Her Eva Gabor went rolling across the grass like a tumble weed. We all stopped dead (bad choice of words, for a cemetery!). We were speechless. I knew how embarrassed Mother was about her hair loss. From that point on, everything seemed to move in slow motion.

And isn't it funny how each personality is clearly displayed when disaster strikes? My daughter, Chera Kay, is so quiet and sensitive. She grabbed Mother's hand and whispered, "It's okay, Nanny. It's okay."

Jacob, my younger nephew, stood motionless with the brightest red face, as if all his grandmother's clothes had been blown off with her hair.

Joshua, the oldest of Mother's grandchildren, is very athletic and very quiet. He simply took off and made the chase across the cemetery to retrieve the rolling bundle.

And my son, Zachary, who does have the slightest tendency to take after his mother, fell to the ground and rolled in the grass laughing. (So much for the strong, sensitive type!)

I certainly wanted to remain sensitive to Mother's embarrassment, but I couldn't help but blurt out, "Hey, Mother, you look like Yoda! I love that movie!" (I told you Zachary was a bit like his mother!)

Mother took off in pursuit (more like a shuffle) behind Joshua. She called out to me over her shoulder, "Are you going to help me or not?" Joshua finally snagged the bundle, turned and handed it to her without even looking up, much like a quarterback making a discreet hand-off. I caught up with her and took hold of one side of the wig as she took the other. Together we pulled it onto her head before any cars could drive by. The once nicely coifed Eva Gabor was now twisted and matted with grass and had lost all its glamour. The name of a certain television evangelist came to mind. (But I didn't say a word! Aren't you proud of me!?)

Mother made her way back to the heart-shaped headstone at Cheralyn's grave. She sat down there, her head in one hand, her arm outstretched and resting against the headstone at Charlotta's grave. Her small, round shoulders were quaking and shaking. *She is so embarrassed,* I thought, feeling bad that I had laughed earlier. *What do I say to her?* Her shoulders were still moving up and down as her grandchildren gathered in close around her. Even Zachary was quiet and concerned now. Finally, she lifted her face, revealing to us not tears of embarrassment but a face that glowed with laughter. She could hardly catch her breath—she was laughing so hard. Her laughter was contagious and one by one we all joined her. "Well, praise the Lord! I guess as long as I can chase my hair, I am alive!" she said.

And we all laughed.

Chonda Pierce

•••

A funeral service was being held for a rather unsavory character who had never been near a place of worship in his life. The services were being conducted by a minister who had never heard of him. Carried away by the occasion, he poured on praise for the departed man.

After ten minutes of hearing the late lamented described as an ideal father, husband, and boss, the widow nudged her son and whispered, "Go up there and make sure it's Papa."

Lowell D. Streiker

•••

3

Dragging Main

Most every city or town has a Main Street—a primary route folks take into, out of, or through town. Dragging Main is part of the town social scene—the place to be part of the "in crowd"—where you can see and be seen.

WALL DRUG

"We might as well close up, Ted," my wife, Dorothy, said. "There won't be any more customers today."

I knew Dorothy was right, but I stepped out into the dusk, hoping to see someone coming our way.

It was December 1931. Dorothy and I had just bought the only drugstore in a town called Wall on the edge of the South Dakota Badlands. We'd been open just a few days, and business had been bad.

I stood shivering on the wooden sidewalk. In this little town there were only 326 people, 326 poor people. Most of them were farmers who'd been wiped out either by the Depression or drought.

Out on the prairie the cold wind whipped up dust devils. I could see a Tin Lizzie chugging along the two-laner. Suitcases were strapped to the running boards. I wished the folks driving would stop, just for a cup of coffee, but they didn't. Here on Main Street no one was out.

I went back inside and turned off the light over the soda fountain. Then I joined Dorothy and our four-year-old son, Billy, in our "apartment," a room we had made by stretching a blanket across the back of the store.

We huddled around the coal stove and waited for our dinner to cook. After Billy was fed and put to bed, Dorothy said to me, "Do you still think this town is the right place for us?"

"I think so," I answered, but I couldn't hide my doubts. It seemed we'd come to a hopelessly bleak place.

I had graduated from pharmacy school in 1929, and after two years of working for other druggists I knew Dorothy and I had to find our own store. My father had left me a three-thousand-dollar legacy. We'd work with that.

We were living in Canova, S.D., when we began our search, covering Nebraska and South Dakota in our Model T. We were sure of two things: We wanted to be in a small town, and we wanted the town to have a Catholic church. In Canova the nearest parish was 20 miles away. We wanted to be able to go to mass every day.

In Wall, where the drugstore was for sale, we found both a small town and a Catholic church. When we talked to the priest, the doctor, and the banker, they all told us Wall was a good place with good people, and they wanted us to come live there.

Dorothy and I were excited about Wall, but when we got back home and told our families about our plan, they were skeptical.

"That town is in the middle of nowhere," a cousin said. "Furthermore, everybody there is flat broke busted."

My father-in-law was understanding, but even he said, "You know, Wall is just about as godforsaken as you can get."

But Dorothy and I couldn't give up on Wall, so our families agreed we should all pray about the decision. In the end everyone felt it was God's will for us to go. But now Dorothy and I wondered if we'd heard God right.

The first few months went by and business didn't improve much. Once again, Dorothy and I sat by the stove and asked ourselves if we'd done the right thing.

"Five years, Dorothy," I said. "That's what I think we should give to this store. If it doesn't work by then, well, then we'll—"

"Don't worry about then," said Dorothy. "We'll make it go. And just think, Ted, pretty soon that monument at Mount Rushmore will be done, and then there will be an endless stream of people going by. I'm sure they'll visit us!"

Over the next few years we drummed up enough business to pay our bills, but that was it. The boys from the Civilian Conservation Corps sometimes came in for sodas on a Saturday night, and every July 10, when Wall held its town birthday, we served a lot of ice cream.

We weren't starving, it's true, and we'd begun to make good friends in Wall. Our pastor, Father John Connolly, had become a tower of strength, helping us keep our faith strong. And we had worked hard to serve our neighbors well. Filling prescriptions for a sick child or an ailing farmer made me feel I was doing something good. I also studied some veterinary medicine on my own so I could help out farmers when their stock was ill.

But all this didn't seem to be enough. Maybe, as Dorothy's father had said, Wall was godforsaken.

By the time the summer of 1936 came around, our business hadn't grown much at all. Our five-year trial would be up in December. What would we do then? Along with nine-year-old Billy, Dorothy and I now had a one-month-old daughter, Mary Elizabeth. What hardships were they in for? I was lost in a dust storm of worries and doubts. I was ready to give up.

One Sunday, though, in the deadening heat of a July afternoon, Dorothy said, "You don't need me here, Ted. I'm going to go put Billy and the baby down for a nap and maybe take one myself." So she and the children headed off to a room we had rented on the outskirts of town.

I minded the empty store. I swatted flies with a rolled-up newspaper. I stood in the door, and no matter where I looked, there was no shade, because the sun was so high and fierce.

An hour later Dorothy came back.

"Too hot to sleep?" I asked.

"No, it wasn't the heat," Dorothy said. "It was all the cars going by on Route 16A. The jalopies just about shook the house to pieces."

"That's too bad," I said.

"No, because you know what, Ted? I think I finally saw how we can get all those travelers to come to our store."

"How's that?" I asked.

"Well, what is it those travelers really want after driving across that hot prairie? They want water. Ice cold water! Why don't we put up signs on the highway telling people to come here for free ice water? Listen, I even made up a few lines for the sign:

"Get a soda
  Get a root beer
    Turn next corner
      Just as near
        To Highway 16 and 14
          Free ice water
            Wall Drug"

Dragging Main 51

It wasn't Wordsworth, but I was willing to give it a try. During the next few days a high-school boy and I put together some signs. We modeled them after the Burma Shave highway signs. Each phrase of Dorothy's little poem went on a 12- by 36-inch board.

The next weekend the boy and I went out to the highway and put up our signs. We spaced the boards out so people could read them as they drove. I must admit I felt somewhat silly doing it, but by the time I got back to the store people were already showing up for their ice water.

Dorothy was running all around to keep up. I pitched in alongside her. For hours people came pouring in, all hot and frazzled. For hours we poured gallons if ice water, made ice cream cones, and gave directions. We ran through our supply of cracked ice. I began chiseling more off the block.

When the day was done, Dorothy and I were pooped. We sat in front of the store, watching the sun set, feeling a cool breeze come in off the prairie. In the summer twilight Wall looked radiant. It looked like a great place to call home.

"Well, Ted," Dorothy said after a while, "I guess the ice water signs worked."

They surely did, and we've never been lonely for customers since. The following summer we had to hire eight girls to help us, and now that the store is in the good hands of my son, Bill, Wall Drug draws up to 20,000 people on a good summer day.

Free ice water. It brought us Husteads a long way, and it taught me my greatest lesson: There's absolutely no place on God's earth that's godforsaken. No matter where you live, you can succeed, because you can reach out to other people with something they need.

And when you give people what they need, you've helped them. You'll find that when you help others, you end up helping yourself as well. That means more than good business; it means a good, happy life.

Ted Hustead

HIGHWAY HANGUPS

A lady whose husband had just bought a new car persuaded him to let her try it out while he drove off to work in the old clunker they were keeping for her. She glided around town with the utmost care, as all new car owners do, until it was time to meet her husband downtown for lunch. As she pulled into his office parking lot, her foot missed the brake pedal and there was a heart-rending crunch of metal. She crawled out, gloomily surveying the accordion pleats in her fender, and said to the parking attendant, "How on earth will I ever tell my husband about this?" Then she took a good look at the car she had smashed into. It was the old clunker.

Art Linkletter

Bumper Sticker Wisdom

Two wrongs don't make a right, but two Wrights made an airplane.

It's not the pace of life that concerns me; it's the sudden stop at the end.

The problem with the gene pool is that there is no lifeguard.

Living on Earth is expensive, but it does include a free trip around the sun every year.

The only time the world beats a path to your door is if you're in the bathroom.

If God wanted me to touch my toes, he would have put them on my knees.

Never knock on Death's door. Ring the doorbell and run. He hates that.

Lead me not into temptation. I can find the way myself.

Jim Kraus

••

The drive-in bank was established so that the real owner of a car could get to see it once in a while.
Great Quotations, Inc.

••

ENTERING CONVENIENTVILLE
—
AN ENTIRELY DRIVE-THRU COMMUNITY!

ZIGGY © ZIGGY AND FRIENDS, INC. Reprinted with permission of UNIVERSAL PRESS SYNDICATE. All rights reserved.

FUMBLING IN THE DARK

The tire blew out on a pitch-black country road, with the rain coming down in freezing gusts. Without an umbrella or raincoat, my friend stepped into the downpour to get his jack out of the trunk. His flashlight was gone. Somehow he managed to fumble the jack into position, unable to see a thing, got the car jacked up, and changed the tire. His hands were skinned and numb with cold, but at last the job was done. With chattering teeth, he crawled back in the car, stepped on the gas—and heard an ominously familiar "thump, thump, thump"! He crawled back out to check the trouble, and I shall spare you his exact words as he saw that he had changed the wrong tire.

Art Linkletter

• •

Billy Graham tells of a time early in his ministry when he arrived in a small town to preach. Wanting to mail a letter, he asked a young boy where the post office was. When the boy had told him, Dr. Graham thanked him and said, "If you'll come to the church this evening, you can hear me telling everyone how to get to Heaven."

I don't think so," the boy said. "You don't even know your way to the post office."

The World's Best Bathroom Book
• •

YOU CAN'T DO THAT!

Sulphur Springs, Texas, where my parents live, has one of those famous old Texas "squares" in the middle of downtown. It's called a square because there are stores on four sides of a big open area that's as big as a city block. The open area is a huge parking lot in the center with a one-way street that goes completely around it next to the stores. It's a bit like venturing onto an English traffic roundabout, with traffic coming in at all four corners of the square, and traveling around the square until you get to the street where you need to exit. The entire area—street and parking lot—is paved with hand-laid bricks.

On the northeast corner of the square is a gorgeous, three-story, one-hundred-and-twenty-year-old courthouse made of a pinkish stone, oval windows, a domed roof, and little cupolas here and there. A truly authentic piece of Texas tradition and American nostalgia.

The square is the center of city activity. Regardless of where you're trying to go, you most always end up on the square at some point. And navigating the traffic on the square is entertaining, to say the least.

One busy Saturday morning, an old fella came into town from his place in the country to get a haircut and do his Saturday shopping. He was in an original Model T Ford, which he guided proudly into the traffic on the square. But about half way around the square, he decided he didn't want to *be* on the square; so he stuck his hand out the window indicating he was going to make a U-turn right in the middle of the one-way traffic.

Seeing what he was about to do, a policeman directing traffic yelled, "Hey, mister! You can't do that!"

The old man stopped, poked his head out the window, took a good look around, and yelled back, "Yeah, I think I can make it!" Then he proceeded to wind up that old Ford and drove upstream through the traffic back to the place where he'd come in and headed back to the country.

The policeman was so shocked and amused that he just let him go and stood there in the middle of the square laughing his head off.

Clyde Shrode
as told to his daughter, Mary Hollingsworth

Two tourists were driving through Louisiana. As they were approaching Natchitoches, they started arguing about the pronunciation of the town. They argued back and forth until they stopped for lunch. As they stood at the counter, one tourist asked the gal at the cash register, "Before we order, could you please settle an argument for us? Would you please pronounce where we are . . . very slowly?" The young woman leaned over the counter and said, "Burrrrrrrr, gerrrrr, Kiiiing."

Lowell D. Streiker

THE FIDDLE

Ross Foley was sitting among some old oil cans in his filling station at Jewett the afternoon I sought him out to talk about country music. He stopped what he was doing immediately, reached for a battered black case, and carefully drew out of it an ancient fiddle.

"No, sir," he said, lightly thumbing the strings, "there's not enough money in that Jewett bank to buy this fiddle. It belonged to my daddy, Uncle Tom Foley, and it was given to him by Bob Wills."

Uncle Tom Foley has been dead since 1957, but in the world of what fiddlers and guitar pickers refer to as Texas breakdown music, Uncle Tom's name won't ever fade. He was champion fiddler of Texas for fifteen years and seldom came out second best in a contest.

"When Bob Wills was just a youngster," Foley said, taking his father's old bow out of the case, "my daddy gave him the first fiddle he ever owned. Bob's mother and my daddy were brother and sister. Bob was born over at Kosse, I think it was, but the Willses lived out here about ten miles in the country till Bob was a big kid and then they moved to Memphis."

While he talked, Ross drew Uncle Tom's bow experimentally across the fiddle strings. "Well, after Bob had made good in country and western music, along about in the late 1920s he came to my daddy and he said, 'Uncle Tom, you gave me my first fiddle, and you helped me and I want to do something for you.' So he gave him this very fiddle. What it's worth I wouldn't guess. I figure it must be over a hundred years old."

There was a honk out on the driveway of the filling station. A customer had driven in and Foley hadn't noticed. He called out the front door, "Just help yourself to whatever you want. I'm kind of busy now."

So while the customer helped himself to a tank of gas, Ross Foley set his foot to patting and the bow to sawing, and out came a nice chorus of "Leather Britches." And then some of "Take Me Back to Texas" and a bit of "Tom and Jerry," the tune Uncle Tom Foley played to win so many of his contests.

I looked down and saw my own foot patting and my pencil keeping time on the edge of the notebook. A funny thing, I never was very high on country and western and breakdown music. I always preferred something I considered more sophisticated, and I ran around Texas for years before I paid much attention to the great influence that fiddle music has on country and small-town Texans. It has to rank as the true folk music of Texas, the music of the great majority of the people. Sure, in Houston and Dallas there are thousands who dance to popular music and dress up and attend symphony concerts, and likely these people would snort at the idea that country music is the music of the people of this state. But they just haven't ever driven down a highway on Saturday night and counted the country dance spots, crowded to the rafters with people lured out by fiddle sawing and guitar picking. I'd bet that among Texans who take an active interest in music, there are ten country and western fans to each person who prefers popular or classical fare. I can't prove that. I just bet that way.

I discovered you can't appreciate country music just by listening to it on radio or television. You've got to be there, where it's being produced, and sit and watch as well as listen. I learned the same thing about Mexican music. Thousands of Texans have a grudge against Mexican music because they grew up in those years when the best available entertainment consisted of listening to *Amos 'n' Andy* and *Fibber McGee and Molly* on radio. About the time Fibber would open his closet and you'd lean close to the speaker to hear all the contents spill out in that grand and noisy way, your station would fade and get overpowered by some Mexican signal. And instead of hearing Fibber's closet empty itself you'd hear a bunch of Mexicans singing and guitaring and spitting out words so fast you couldn't understand them even if you made A in textbook Spanish.

I really hated the sound of Mexican singers until I started going to Mexico. Then a friend who lives down there taught me that just listening to Mexican singers, as on radio or a record, is something different from watching them sing. It's the difference between bitter and sweet. I've ended up a nut about mariachi bands, and when I go to Mexico I spend many more pesos than are prudent hiring them to sing. It's the same music I used to cuss in the Fibber McGee days.

The tunes Ross Foley played in his filling station that day were also the ones I used to sneer at, along with all my high-school associates, when we thought the only music worth listening to was played by Tommy Dorsey and Glenn Miller.

But if you can sit there in Foley's service station, or anywhere else, and watch him saw away at "Leather Britches" and "Take Me Back to Texas" and fail to pat your foot, then you were born with a stone ear. That's when you learn about country music, and why so many people love it and why it's such a great part of the entertainment of rural people.

Country music has a way of becoming family tradition,

and families often take pride in the fact that all the members are musical. The Foleys at Jewett are this way. Uncle Tom Foley had three brothers, all musicians. There was Blue-Eye Foley, whose first name was George but who went by the nickname because he had one blue eye and one brown, and there was Uncle Jim Foley, then Feely Foley, all fiddlers.

It's difficult for an outsider to grasp the hold that music has on true country entertainers. "You know," Ross Foley said, finishing his fiddling there in the filling station, "I can remember my daddy getting up at two o' clock in the morning, building a fire in the stove and fiddlin' until daylight, whether there was anybody listening or not." He laid the old fiddle reverently back in its case. "Music was just in him," Ross said, "and it had to come out."

Leon Hale

"My name is Leonard, and I'll be your auto mechanic for today."

© The New Yorker Collection 1992. George Booth from cartoonbank.com. All Rights Reserved.

You Might Be from a Small Town If:

You can name everyone you graduated with.

You get a whiff of manure and think of home.

You know what 4-H is.

You ever went to "headlight parties."

You used to drag "Main."

You said a bad word and your parents knew within the hour.

You ever went cow-tipping.

School gets cancelled for state sporting events.

You could never buy cigarettes because all the store clerks knew how old you were (and, if you were old enough, they'd tell your parents, anyhow).

You were ever in the Homecoming parade.

You have ever gone home for Homecoming.

You fix up to go buy milk lest anyone starts the rumor that you have gained weight or quit taking care of yourself.

No place sells gas on Sunday.

Friday night fun consisted of standing in line for the one-screen theater, and since it was sold out, watching truckers and drinking coffee at the truck stop (the only place open after ten).

You have to drive an hour to buy a pair of socks.

It was cool to date someone from the neighboring town.

You have ever gone for a walk in the cemetery on a date.

You ordered your wardrobe out of a catalog.

You had senior skip day.

The whole school went to the same party after graduation. You don't give directions by street names or house numbers, but you give directions by references (turn by Armstrongs', go two blocks past Andersons', and it's four houses left of the track field).

Compiled from various sources

MISS ANNIE

My notion is that the day Miss Annie Spinn died was a sad one for the little city of Brenham. The town lost a heavy touch of color with Miss Annie's passing.

On one of my earliest visits to Brenham I saw Miss Annie pull up in front of a drugstore and double-park. Double-parking on the courthouse square is normally frowned on by Brenham police, but they permitted Miss Annie to park where she pleased. Anyway, she could hardly park head-in, because she drove a sorrel mare hitched to a buggy. This wasn't in 1915, now. Miss Annie was still driving that mare in the early 1960s. She had been coming to town in the buggy so many years that gray-haired people around town couldn't remember when she hadn't.

There in front of the drugstore Miss Annie collared the first passer-by and issued orders for him to go in and send out a clerk. Miss Annie expected curb service and she got it. She also got the right-of-way on all streets no matter which way she headed or turned, and there was an unwritten traffic law in Brenham that everybody was supposed to watch out for Miss Annie Spinn. She was apt to execute a U-turn at just about any intersection, even right there on the courthouse square, and you had better look sharp to miss her.

In her late years Miss Annie's eyesight wasn't much good, and the sorrel mare's wasn't either. I always thought it spoke well of the people of Brenham, the way they watched out for Miss Annie and her mare.

I stopped a traffic officer and asked him if it ever occurred to the police department to give Miss Annie a ticket for her violations. He said no.

Then I eased over to the corner where the drugstore clerk had answered Miss Annie's summons. She wanted a bulb for her flashlight. The clerk went back in and brought out a bulb. It wasn't the right size so he went back in and brought out another. Miss Annie looked that one over, thought about it awhile, and decided not to buy the bulb. Just didn't like it. So she spoke to the mare, which wheeled around and pulled the buggy through a U-turn and trotted off through the downtown traffic on the wrong side of the street.

A few months after that I went to Brenham hoping to talk to Miss Annie, and got directed out north of town, where she was seen headed a few minutes earlier. I caught the buggy just as the mare was pulling it off the pavement onto the dirt road that leads to Miss Annie's old home three miles outside town.

I'm pretty sure Miss Annie was asleep when I drove up beside the buggy. They say she often took naps while riding, but it didn't really matter because the mare knew where Miss Annie was going anyway and could see better than her mistress and didn't need any steering.

Miss Annie's brown little weathered face lighted up considerably when I finally got her stopped and asked a question or two. A three-gallon cream can was at her feet. For goodness knows how many years she just brought cream to the creamery. I asked her that day if she ever had any trouble with the traffic in town.

"No-o-o-o," she said, "not a bit."

But didn't anybody ever complain about the buggy and the mare being on the streets?

"Well, there was one fellow that complained one time, and when I heard it I went straight to the chief of police and asked him if it was all right if I kept coming to town. And he said I could come to town in this buggy just whenever I pleased. I've been paying taxes in Washington County longer than anybody that's complaining about my buggy. I've got to go now. I'm pretty busy. It's been mighty dry out on my place and I've had to haul water from town every day." She spoke to the mare and the buggy moved off, leaving me standing there in the road with a lot more questions to ask.

Miss Annie lived alone on that farm until she was well up into her eighties, and then she had to go to a rest home, where she died. Shortly before she had to leave home I was passing through Brenham and there was Miss Annie double-parked in front of the post office, waiting for somebody to bring out her mail. She got curb service at the post office just the same as she did at the drugstore. The town has not been nearly so interesting since she's gone.

Leon Hale

···

This old rancher in Montana hates wearing a seat belt, but one day he's driving on the highway with his wife and sees a state patrol car behind him, and he says to his wife, "Quick, take the wheel! I gotta put my seat belt on!" So she does, and right then the patrolman pulls them over. He walks up to the car and he says, "Say, I noticed you weren't wearing your seat belt."

The rancher says, "I was too, but you don't have to take my word for it—my wife here is a good Christian woman, ask her; she'll tell you the truth. She doesn't lie about anything."

The cop says to the wife, "So? How about it, ma'am?" And the wife says: "I've been married to

Buck for twenty years, officer, and one thing I've learned in all that time is this: you never argue with him when he's drunk."

Garrison Keillor

"WHAT DOES A FELLA HAFTA DO TO GET A SPEEDIN' TICKET AROUND HERE?"

Our small mountain church is located by a frequently-traveled road. Sometimes during services, the church PA system picks up CB broadcasts from passing motorists. The CB'ers, of course, are unaware that their voices are being heard in a meeting. Once, the pastor began a prayer, saying, "O Lord, we beseech you to meet our various needs . . ." Suddenly he was interrupted by a loud voice that crackled over the PA, "I'll be right on down!"

Rusty Wright and Linda Raney Wright

Slow Down

Have you ever watched kids on a merry-go-round, or listened to the rain slapping on the ground?

Ever followed a butterfly's erratic flight, or gazed at the sun into the fading night?

You better slow down, don't dance so fast, time is short, the music won't last.

Do you run through each day on the fly? When you ask, "How are you?" Do you hear the reply?

When the day is done, do you lie in your bed, with the next hundred chores running through your head?

You'd better slow down, don't dance so fast, time is short, the music won't last.

Ever told your child, we'll do it tomorrow, and in your haste, not seen his sorrow?

Ever lost touch, let a good friendship die, 'cause you never had time to call and say "Hi"?

You'd better slow down, don't dance so fast, time is short, the music won't last.

When you run so fast to get somewhere, you miss half the fun of getting there.

When you worry and hurry through your day, it is like an unopened gift . . . thrown away.

Life is not a race, do take it slower. Hear the music, before the song is over.

Author Unknown

••

I moved recently to Cottonwood, California, a town so small it only has two streets in it—Main Street and Non-Main Street.

Lowell D. Streiker

••

4

Over the Back Fence

Cats caterwauling, dogs howling, parents calling kids, the aroma of steaks on the grill, lawn mowers running, kids laughing—over the back fence are the sounds and smells of life in your neighborhood.

IT'S A DOG'S LIFE, BUT LAUGH ANYWAY

I'm convinced some things happen to us for the sheer comedy of it all—you know, so life doesn't get boring. Like any good drama, life has to have a bit of comic relief to ease the tension and rejuvenate our spirits.

Take the time my husband did some work for one of our neighbors. He didn't expect any remuneration, but the man insisted on giving him a "little something" to show his appreciation. That little something turned out to be his full-grown, purebred pit bull. The dog came with papers, a month's supply of food, and incisors the size of the Washington Monument!

My husband tried his best to convince the man that a simple

thank you was enough. After all, that pit bull was *his* dog, a part of *his* family.

We couldn't bring him into our backyard. His home was next door. We knew that, our neighbor knew that, and that tank with teeth knew that. But pit bulls have a reputation for being very territorial. As soon as he got used to our backyard, the owner explained, he'd be a wonderful watchdog, protecting our home as well as he had his own. All we had to do was give the animal time.

As it turned out, he didn't need much time. Within fifteen minutes he proved to be the perfect watchdog. The only problem was that he was protecting our home from *us!*

Our backyard became a mere extension of his, and we weren't even allowed back there! All day long Shredder (we took the liberty of renaming him) would pace back and forth by our sliding glass window, growling, snarling, double daring us to open it. To feed him, we had to wait until he was on the other side of the yard, open a window, toss out some meat, and close it again before his snapping jaws could get there.

This went on for about a week. We were prisoners in our own home. That dog owned the place. He wasn't making the payments to the mortgage company. He wasn't paying the utilities (although he did help bring down the electric bill by chewing through several wires). He wasn't helping us maintain the house in any way, but it was HIS house!

Our lawn chair became his throne, and our limbs were the chew toy of his dreams. All day long he'd stare at us through the windows, stalking our every move, waiting for the slightest slipup—a door left ajar, an unsecured window, an open screen. We could hear his breathing through the air-conditioning vents. We watched him growl at our shadows. Even the holes he dug made us nervous. They were rectangular and looked remarkably like burial plots.

In short, it wasn't working out. One of us had to find

another place to live, and since he had less furniture to move, we decided it should be him.

Luckily, the telephone wires were still intact, so we called our neighbor and politely asked him to come over and repossess his dog.

We were tired of being pushed around by that four-legged battering ram with bad breath. We were fed up with paying for a backyard we weren't able to use. We had had enough of that canine bully leaving teeth marks in our stucco and trying to "fetch" the mailman. We were determined to give the dog back if we had to Federal Express him back!

Our neighbor was gracious, yet disappointed. He felt we were giving up prematurely. He thought we should give the dog more time to get used to us. After all, we still had most of our fingers left. Time would help us to emotionally connect. It would allow us to win over his loyalty. It would force us to bond.

But we didn't budge. The only bonding we wanted was with our backyard again—without having an ambulance on standby.

Eventually, the owner felt sorry enough for us that he let the dog return home. Until the day we moved, however, I don't think Shredder ever forgave us for continuing to live on "his" property. As far as he was concerned, we were trespassers, and it was his job to let everyone within city limits know it—twenty-four hours a day.

But that's all right. Thanks to all his barking, we didn't have to buy an alarm clock for years. He also taught us that it truly *is* better to give back than to receive.

Martha Bolton

....

A good neighbor is a fellow who smiles at you over the back fence, but doesn't climb over it.
Arthur Baer

....

70 Main Street Mirth

A tourist stopped at a country gas station. While his car was being serviced, he noticed an old-timer basking in the sun with a piece of rope in his hand. The tourist walked up to the old-timer and asked, "What do you have there?"

"That's a weather gauge, sonny," the old-timer replied.

"How can you possibly tell the weather with a piece of rope?"

"It's simple," said the old-timer. "When it swings back and forth, it's windy. And when it gets wet, it's raining."

Bob Phillips

He was asking the editor of a small-town weekly paper how they ever kept in business. Subscriptions, job printing, and advertising helped some, admitted the editor, but the thing that kept them in the black was selling their typographical errors to the humor departments of big city dailies.

The Public Speaker's Handbook of Humor

A garage sale is a technique for distributing all the junk in your garage among all the other garages in the neighborhood.

Bob Phillips

THE PANTRY

In my memories of long ago, most houses had a pantry off the kitchen. The kitchens were large and roomy, but the pantries were small and compact, often no more than six feet wide by eight or ten feet in length. Grandma and Mom spent a great deal of time scurrying back and forth across our huge kitchen as they prepared meals for the family—the sink was at one end of the room, the icebox at the other end, and the wood stove and kitchen cabinets quite a distance from the kitchen table, where food was usually prepared. But in the pantry, space was limited, with every inch used to advantage—few steps were required to prepare a batch of bread dough, churn the butter, or stir up a pitcher of pancake batter. Cabinets with handy workspace on top surrounded the little room, and ingredients and utensils waited right at your fingertips.

A pantry was a mother's paradise. Luscious pies were rolled out, put together, baked in the wood stove in the kitchen, and then whisked back into the pantry to cool until suppertime; birthday cakes were magically decorated and stored away on pantry shelves for safekeeping, to be presented later at a birthday celebration along with a freezer full of homemade ice cream that Mom had hidden away in the pantry beneath a layer of ice and several coverings of feed bags.

A pantry was often the core of family life. The grandmothers, mothers, and daughters frosted cakes, mixed up cookies, and made biscuits and doughnuts as they talked with one another side by side in the pantry's tight quarters. Girls giggled and exchanged ideas and consoled one another as they nibbled on goodies from the bread box or perhaps freshly baked cupcakes or cookies from a tray. Little boys' and girls' hurts soon seemed much better after some tender loving care from Mom and a visit to the pantry for a special treat.

From time to time, the pantry became a kind of sanctuary where one could escape to find solace and renewed strength when life's burdens seemed too heavy to bear. In the beloved pantry, tears and sadness were soon replaced by hope and contentment in the presence of the past year's harvest: row upon row of quart and pint jars filled with shimmering preserves and jellies rested in the sparkling sunshine that streamed through the windows. Their beautiful colors gleamed like jewels. A full larder was a house well blessed.

In days gone by, the pantry was the center of life and family. It held not only food for the body but also nourishment for the spirit. Perhaps someday my modern, rural home will be equipped with a pantry off the kitchen, just like those in my memories of long ago, when a pantry added charm to my childhood home.

Helen Colwell Oakley

PERSPECTIVE

Today I stood at my window and cursed the pouring rain,
Today a desperate farmer prayed for his fields of grain.
My weekend plans are ruined, it almost makes me cry
While the farmer lifts his arms and blesses the clouded sky.
The alarm went off on Monday and I cursed my work routine,
Next door a laid-off mechanic feels the empty pockets of his jeans.
I can't wait for my vacation, some time to take for me,
He doesn't know tonight how he'll feed his family.
I cursed my leaky roof and the grass I need to mow,
A homeless man downtown checks for change in the telephone.
I need a new car, mine is getting really old,
He huddles in a doorway, seeking shelter from the cold.
With blessings I'm surrounded, the rain, a job, a home,
Though my eyes are often blinded by the things I think I own.

J. John and Mark Stibbe

"See? I told you our yard was too small for a swing set."

CORDIALITY

Of all human traits, I believe cordiality to be my favorite. That warmth of greeting, that enthusiasm which makes everyone, friend or stranger, feel welcomed, wanted, liked, and enjoyed.

Maybe this is partly because I was lucky enough to grow up neighbors to some people named the Johnsons. What the house lacked in luxuries it more than made up for in this rich quality. You felt it like a gift, a kind of happy bestowal, the minute any one of its members opened the door.

"Well, come in, come in. Say, but it's great to see you—hey, Dad (or Babe or Jack or Lois)—look who's here!"

It made you feel special, that greeting. It made you feel like someone they'd actually been hoping for. Nor did this cozy, glowing sensation leave, no matter how long you stayed. They talked with you, they laughed with you, they focused their attention upon you with interest and warmth and joy. And they never seemed to want you to go. "Ah, come on—listen, you just got here. Wait now, have another cup of coffee, let's talk some more."

That everyone who entered got the same treatment didn't diminish the value of your own reception a bit. You knew, somehow, that they were sincere—they did enjoy people. All kinds of people, attractive or not so attractive, rich or poor. Cordiality was not just something assumed out of kindness or courtesy, it was unconscious, spewing naturally out of an innate delight in human fellowship. Therefore you accepted it, trusted it, knew with an overwhelming certitude that, whatever your own shortcomings, you were truly welcome here.

Cordiality . . . Cordially yours . . . It is not a lost art; there are many who still practice it, if only because it's their nature, they can't help it. Yet I wonder sometimes if sheer old-fashioned cordiality hasn't gone out of style? People so seldom sign letters "cordially" anymore. The occupants of some homes seem to have lost the hang of it. Despite the perfunctory courtesies, even some of the most excessive attentions, you feel uncomfortable. As if, "I shouldn't have come," or "I mustn't stay long," or "How soon can I politely leave?"

What a pity! Doorbells were meant for ringing. Houses for the entry as well as the departure of visitors. True, often we are so harried, preoccupied with personal concerns, that the unexpected arrival of some caller is not a thing of joy.

And yet . . . if we could only all be Johnsons. Able to sing out, and truly mean it, "Well, come in, come in—look who's here!" And, "Oh, stay just a little longer, it's so good to see you, please don't go." Our own hearts would be the richer.

Marjorie Holmes

•••

A woman went into a small town post office recently and asked for five dollars worth of stamps.

"What denomination?" asked the clerk.

"Well," came the angry reply, "I didn't know it would ever come to this. But if the nosy government people have to know, I'm a Baptist!"

Bob Phillips

•••

GETTING RID OF ANTS IS NO PICNIC

I was visiting the folks in Moreland, Georgia, and my stepfather, H. B., and I walked out into the front yard.

Over near the driveway, I noticed a couple of large anthills.

"I've tried everything I know to get rid of these ants," said my stepfather. "I even put grits on them."

For a second, I thought he had said he put grits on the ants, but you'd have to be about half-addled to do something like that, and H.B. is, without doubt, of sound mind.

I know a lot about grits. I know they are misunderstood. The reason people from regions other than the South don't like grits is they have never had them prepared properly.

They are traveling through the South and stop at a HoJo for breakfast and the waitress serves them grits with their eggs and bacon.

They're probably instant grits to begin with, and I'm sure it's in the Bible somewhere that instant grits are an unholy hybrid of the real thing.

Also, our travelers don't know to put butter on their grits and then stir their eggs and bacon into them and salt and pepper to taste.

So their grits taste awful. And when they return home, they are asked, "Did you have any grits?"

And they say, "The worst thing we ever ate. Almost ruined our trip to Disney World."

Putting grits on ant beds is an old remedy for getting rid of ants.

But grits on an anthill?

"You didn't really put grits on these ant beds, did you?" I said to my stepfather.

"That's exactly what I said. Putting grits on ant beds is an old remedy for getting rid of ants."

"Giving Northerners unbuttered instant grits is an old remedy for getting rid of tourists, too," I said.

"What's supposed to happen," H. B. went on, "is the ants try to eat the individual little grits and they get so full they explode and die."

"I've heard of other old remedies. I know if you put tobacco juice on a bee sting, it will quit hurting.

I know to put a pork chop around an ugly child's neck to get the dogs to play with him, and I know if you bury a dishrag under a full moon your warts will go away.

But, again, grits on an anthill?
So I asked, "How are the grits working on the ants?"
"These ants," answered H. B., don't seem to be interested in grits."
"Aha!" I said. "They're Northern ants."
"How do you know?"
"Elementary," I said. "They refuse to eat grits, and look how many of them are wearing sandals with black socks."
I told my stepfather not to worry about the ants. They'd be on their way to Disney World in a matter of days.

Lewis Grizzard

•••

The local orchestra was playing with great feeling, "Carry Me Back to Old Virginia." A man at a table in the corner was weeping. Touched, the leader went over to console him. "Are you a Virginian?" asked he.
    "No—I'm a musician," replied the weeper.

James Wesley Jackson

•••

THE ONE AND ONLY VIDALIA ONION

Whenever I am confronted by atheists, I simply make the point that if there wasn't a God and He didn't love us, there wouldn't be such a thing as the beloved Vidalia onion.
    Think about it: Vidalia onions, which are sweet and mild, grow only in a small part of southeast Georgia.
    Some have tried to duplicate the Vidalia in other parts of the country, but to no avail.
    God, I am convinced, was traveling through what was to

become southeast Georgia during the six days of Creation and said, "Let there be a sweet, mild onion, and let it grow here and here only."

It was just another of the many blessings God gave us, such as spring, cool breezes, the beach, and frequent-flyer points.

I must admit, however, that I have had a problem with Vidalia onions over the years. I usually buy them in great quantities.

I am afraid if I don't, the Arabs will get control of Vidalias and send the price up so far I can't buy them anymore.

My problem is that I can't eat my onions fast enough, and some of my supply turns funny colors and begins to smell.

Because I absolutely abhor throwing out spoiled Vidalia onions, I set about to find a way to keep them fresh for long periods of time.

Finally, I have the answer.

Friends invited me to dinner recently, and delicious baked Vidalia onions were served.

During the meal, I asked, "Do you have a problem keeping your Vidalias fresh?"

"Of course not," the husband answered. "I've got fifty pounds of them stored right now. I'll be eating Vidalia onions all winter. The best way to keep Vidalias," he went on, "is to put them in panty hose."

"Panty hose?"

"Yes," the wife explained. "You take a pair of panty hose and cut off the top part.

"Then you put an onion all the way to the place where your foot goes. Then you tie a knot just above that onion and put in another on top of it. When the panty hose are full of onions, you hang them up somewhere and they stay absolutely fresh.

"What you are doing is keeping the onions from touching one another, which is one reason they go bad if you leave them stored in, say, a sack."

"I hope you don't mind if I tell the rest of the nation about this," I said to my friends.

"Fine, but I don't believe you should mention us by name," said the husband while his wife was not in the room.

"It could be a little embarrassing if you wrote that my wife could get fifty pounds of Vidalia onions in a pair of her panty hose."

I put my hand on what was left of my baked Vidalia and swore I would be discreet.

Lewis Grizzard

"Forget lemonade. The real money's in bottled water."

© www.CartoonStock.com

••

There isn't much to be seen in a little town, but what you hear makes up for it.

Kin Hubbard

••

5

Front Pages and Front Porches

The local newspaper is the go-to source for a city or town's news and notes. And the headlines on the front page are history (or perhaps hysterics) in the making, all told and retold on the front porches around town.

MEBBE THE FRONT PORCH SHOULD COME BACK

I was driving through the outskirts of the city the other day, and I saw a man sitting on a front porch.

It was an older house and he was an older man. Modern houses don't have front porches anymore, and even if they did, younger men have far too much to do to sit on them.

I'm not certain when the front porch all but disappeared from American life, but it probably was about the same time television and air conditioning were being installed in most every home.

Why sit out on the porch where it's hot and you can get mosquito bit when you can sit inside where it's comfort-cooled and watch *Ozzie and Harriet?*

Even if an architect designs a porch today, it's usually placed in the back of the house where the hot tub is.

If we do venture out of our houses today, it's usually to get in the hot tub.

If Americans continue to spend all that time in their hot tubs, we may all eventually shrink down like the Lilliputians and become prunelike from boiling ourselves one too many times.

I grew up in my grandparents' home. They had a front porch; we spent a lot of time sitting on it.

My grandmother would shell butter beans. My grandfather would listen for trains.

"There comes the mail train to Montgomery," he'd say, pulling his watch out of his watch pocket. "She's running four minutes late."

I learned a lot sitting on the front porch with my grandparents. How to shell butter beans. How to find the Big Dipper. How to wait for a mosquito to alight and then slap that sucker dead. What a pleasure it is to listen for trains!

Our neighbors often dropped by and sat on the porch with us.

"It was awful what happened to Norvel Tenny, wasn't it?" a neighbor would say.

"What happened to him?" my grandmother would ask, looking up from her butter beans.

"Got three fingers cut clean off down at the sawmill."

Something else I learned on the front porch—not to include sawmilling in my future.

But even my grandparents eventually moved inside. They bought a television and enclosed the front porch and made it a den.

My grandfather enjoyed westerns. My grandmother never missed a Billy Graham sermon or a televised wrestling match. The mail train to Montgomery had to get along by itself after that.

Perhaps if front porches came back and people started sitting on them again, we'd learn to relax more and talk to one another more, and being bitten by a mosquito would at least be some contact with nature.

I probably should have stopped and talked to the old man on the porch and gotten his opinions on all of this.

I would have, too, but I was late for my tee time.

Lewis Grizzard

THE CRASH OF '89

I was just plain worn out. Maybe the time had come for me to call it quits and give up my drugstore here in Cuthbert. This southern town of ours isn't very large, just 4,000 people or so. We don't even have a traffic light, just a lot of big old houses with rocking chairs on the front porches, and a cluster of shops around a sleepy town square. A little south of there, across the Central of Georgia railroad tracks, Blakely Street dips to a shopping center where you'll find Central Drugs. That's the store I own—and was thinking of selling.

I've been a pharmacist since 1958, living and working in a lot of little towns not unlike Cuthbert. Five years ago I finally bought this store of my own, and my wife, Billie Jean, and I worked hard to get it on a solid footing.

When you work for yourself, you're never really off the job. Take, for instance, one Sunday not long ago: I was getting ready for church when I got a call asking me to drive into town (Billie Jean and I live about eight miles out on Old Lumpkin Road) to fill a prescription that was badly needed.

No sooner had I done that and come back home when the phone rang again. Another request for another prescription, another trip back to town in my pickup. I never got to church that day. I'm not really complaining about it. After all, these are my neighbors, and it's my job, my duty, to help them. But the truth is, at the age of 52 I was just kind of burned out.

There was another reason for my thinking about selling the store. A big chain had offered to buy me out. It was an opportunity to make a bit of money and retire to an easier life. Here was my big chance. Should I take it?

Then came Friday night, January 13. At five minutes after closing time, I was ready to turn out the overhead fluorescent lights. The last customer in the store was waiting for me to prepare an antibiotic suspension for her sick child, but still another customer was on his way over. And I could almost be sure that the special telephone line the doctors used would be ringing any moment to tell me a patient was just leaving the office and heading my way.

I was filling the prescription behind a partition in the back of the store. Billie Jean was there too, going over some schedules with Linda, the new clerk. Out front, Candice, another salesclerk, and Jackie, our store manager, were closing up the cash register.

I looked at my watch. When was that fellow going to show up for his medicine?

The first thing I heard was Jackie yelling, really yelling. And then . . . BAM!

There was a tremendous crash. The floor shook, the walls trembled and dust came down from the ceiling. I hit the floor and covered my head. There was the sound of glass breaking, then the crunch of metal hitting metal.

And then silence.

I stood up and peered out from behind the partition. The front of the store was a mass of twisted metal, powdery rubble and shattered glass. And there, among broken bottles of mouthwash, mangled writing tablets and trembling vitamin capsules, loomed the cab of a three-quarter-ton truck. At the wheel sat the stunned customer I'd been waiting for.

No one seemed to be harmed. Billie Jean stood up, wiping dust out of her eyes. Jackie and Candice came out from behind the drug counter, where they'd leaped when they saw the truck coming. The customer was on the other side of the store, goggle-eyed but safe.

I crunched through the rubble to see about the young man in the truck. There wasn't a scratch on him, but he was mighty shook up. He kept telling me how sorry he was, how his brakes had failed. Then he turned on the motor again, and with more tinkling and grinding and crashing, backed out of the store. As far as I could see, the truck had only two scrapes on it.

I couldn't say the same for Central Drugs. What moments before had been a well-stocked drugstore was now a sea of debris. Pieces of glass from the front window had been propelled 30 feet into the store. The metal shelves had been emptied of toiletries, cold remedies, and stationery supplies. The smell of ammonia, hair conditioner, and nail-polish remover was overwhelming.

A cold winter wind came blasting in through the gaping hole. I went back to the pharmacy counter, where the others stood staring in stunned silence. "Call the police," I said glumly to Billie Jean. "And then call our insurance agent."

Now, almost on cue, the phone on the doctors' line started to ring. I picked up the receiver. "Doc," I said morosely, "you'd better come treat me for a heart attack. A truck just ran into my store."

I looked again at the incredible mess and just turned away. That cinched it. I was getting out of this business once and for all. My wrecked store was the last straw. Almost in a daze, I went back to finishing the antibiotic suspension I'd been working on.

A few minutes later I came out to give the customer her prescription. The police had arrived and were filling out reports with the help of that befuddled driver, whose truck was now out in the parking lot.

I was surprised to find that some friends of ours who live in town, Joan and Wendell Pearson, were in the store. Joan was at work with a broom, sweeping up the glass that had shot clear back to the pharmacy counter. They weren't the only ones, however. More people, customers I recognized, were arriving, asking to be put to work. After the crash had rattled windows blocks away and the doctor on the phone had told his patients, the word had spread throughout town.

Wendell runs Wendell's Auto and Electric, and next thing I knew, his big pickup was backed against the storefront, and folks were loading splintered paneling, twisted aluminum, broken bottles and other debris into it.

Candice's parents arrived. Her father, Sgt. Paul Campbell, an off-duty state trooper, organized people into teams. Someone mustered up carts and boxes, and Jackie explained to people how to sort out the jumbled mess of pencils, hair color, baby powder, and toys.

Ed Pate, a young carpenter, happened to be driving by and offered to build a temporary storefront. In no time, two carpenters and a farmer were measuring distances and laying out tools.

Charles Hardwick, the owner of True Value Hardware next door, appeared with nails and bolts, and Brook Hixon, who owned a building-supply store down the road, brought some two-by-fours and plywood.

In the meantime Wendell hauled off two truckloads of trash and was back for his third. Hammers were pounding and saws were buzzing—a sturdy frame of two-by-fours took shape where the wall and the window used to be.

I tried to count how many people were helping. At this point I think there were about 18—Deanne Wallace, Brenda

Campbell, Ralph Bryant, and Carl Rooks were just a few of them. Some people left to feed their kids but came back to do more, so I couldn't get an exact count.

There was some worry that my burglar alarm system might have been knocked out, so some of my son Robbie's friends volunteered for an all-night stakeout at the store. (It turned out that the city had a portable temporary alarm, so a stakeout wasn't necessary.)

By ten o' clock, the hole in the front of the store was covered by plywood, products were grouped back on the shelves, the floors were swept. The only mess left was a slick of hardened red fingernail polish tracked on the floor and some pieces of glass in the greeting card display, none of which would affect business the next day.

The book of Proverbs says, "Never tell your neighbor to wait until tomorrow if you can help him now" (3:28, GNB). Well, these folks had helped me now all right. They did in four hours what would have taken our staff I don't know how long!

And so it was that The Crash of '89 knocked some sense into me. The next day I told that drugstore chain no thanks. Sure, selling out would have made a big impact on my life in terms of more money and leisure time. But it's nothing like the impact a three-quarter-ton truck—and my good neighbors in Cuthbert—made on me.

A few days ago, about 10 minutes after we'd closed up for the day, a man walked up and tried the door. He didn't knock, but slowly turned to go home. I unlocked the door and called after him, "What do you need, Frank?"

"I need a prescription," he replied, "but you've been here long enough. Just go on home where you belong."

"Come on in," I said, pulling him into the store. "I am where I belong."

Bob Buell

A farmer was quoted in the *Town Gazette* as having "2,008 pigs." He showed up the next morning to declare to the editor, "That's a misprint! I didn't say I have 2,008 pigs. I told your reporter that I have 2 sows and 8 pigs."

Bob Horner

What did the leftovers say when they were put into the freezer?
Foiled again.

Bob Phillips

DELIVERING THE U.S. MAIL

While I was in college, I worked in the campus post office. During the summer break, I landed a special student job with the post office in our town. There were three openings at the local post office, and you had to take a special kind of limited Civil Service exam to qualify. Because I had been working in the postal system for a couple of years, I had more experience than most other students. So I scored a little higher on the test than the other two applicants, and I got to do the "fun" jobs while they had to walk and carry the heavy, leather mail pouch full of mail on their shoulders eighteen miles a day. Not fun. Especially in Texas in July and August.

My job, however, was to drive an official postal truck. Each morning, the postal carriers sorted the mail for their routes, tied it into bundles arranged sequentially by addresses, and put it into mail sacks. They couldn't carry all the mail for their routes for the entire day; so relay boxes had been placed strategically around town, and their sacks of mail had to be placed in those boxes. As soon as the carriers left the post office on foot, following the sequenced mail from house to house, I did what was called "running relays." That meant that I had to beat each one of the carriers to their first relay box, where they picked up their next set of mail, which led them along their routes to the *next* relay box. They continued this procedure all day until their sequenced mail eventually led them back to the post office.

After I ran relays, I then delivered C.O.D.'s, Special Delivery letters, and the like. When I finished those jobs, I delivered parcel post to the downtown businesses. So I was running around all over town every day, not that it was very far from one side of town to the other.

In truth, I was a bit of a novelty in our small town. This was in the late '60s, and in those days very few women worked in the postal system. If they did, they typically worked "the window" selling stamps or sorting mail into postal boxes. They were rarely seen walking a route or driving a postal truck. So people often did a double take when they saw me whizzing down the street in my red-white-and-blue Econoline van. And I took quite a bit of teasing from the mail carriers.

Every day at lunch I met my friend Emily at a burger drive-in. She was still in high school, but we had a lot of fun together.

One day we met for our ritual lunch, and while we were eating, someone tampered with the postal truck I was driving. Of course, it's a federal offense to damage a postal vehicle, punishable by a large fine or imprisonment. So when I discovered their mischief, I didn't know whether to laugh or panic.

On the side where it said "U.S. Mail" someone had crossed out "Mail" and written "Femail."

Mary Hollingsworth

After a long evening of conversation the host said, "I hate to put you out, but I have to get up at six o'clock in the morning to catch a plane."

"Good heavens," said the guest. "I thought you were at my house!"

Bob Phillips

"No, no. He's ceramic. He just fools real burglars into thinking our house has already been hit."

Rebecca's House Rules (at least one fits any occasion).
1. Throw it on the bed.
2. Fry onions.
3. Call Jenny's mother.

4. No one's got the corner on suffering.
5. Run it under the cold tap.
6. Everything takes practice, except being born.

Sharon Mathews

MAMA AND THE SILVER COMET

My 10-year-old granddaughter's mouth is a sudden O. "Nanny, can I try this dress on? I've never seen such a wonderful dress in my whole life!"

Jamie is spending the night, and she'd been looking through my clothes closet when she came upon the formal. That unforgettable dress! As I help Jamie into it, I think back to the time I first tried it on . . . and to the time I started off to that special dance without it. How I had worried about that dress! Suddenly the memories come—easily, vividly, sweetly . . .

I'd recently started my first job in Atlanta, and I often went home to Elberton, 100 miles east. A few weeks earlier a hometown boy I'd been dating, Jerry West, who was attending Virginia Polytechnic Institute, had asked my mother, eyeball to eyeball, "Would you let Marion come up to V.P.I. for our big dance weekend? Fats Domino is going to be there. I'd get her a nice room with a little lady who rents rooms. She could ride the Silver Comet."

I couldn't imagine my mother allowing me to do such a thing. It was 1957 and most young girls I knew didn't go off unchaperoned for a weekend. But I knew she liked Jerry.

Jerry waited, still looking right into Mama's eyes. I glanced back and forth apprehensively. Both of them smiled ever so slightly. "I don't see why not," Mama said. My mouth opened and Jerry lit up as if a light had gone on inside him. We went to the train station right then and got my ticket.

Mama wanted me to have a new formal. I'd worked as a secretary for a few months since I'd been out of college, but didn't have any extra money. She said I could select a dress and charge it to her. She assured me she'd have it paid for quickly. Mama had worked at the Granite City Bank since my father died, when I was two. She managed her modest salary well. "Get something really pretty, Mannie," she added.

I'd planned to look all over Atlanta until I found the perfect dress. Unbelievably, I discovered it almost immediately on my lunch hour. I went to one of the finest stores in the city, a small, exclusive store I'd never been in before. There it was! My dress. I stood mesmerized, not even hearing what the saleslady said to me in a nasal voice. She repeated, louder, "May I help you?"

Without taking my eyes off the dress, I said in hushed tones, "I want that dress." It was on a mannequin. My colors: champagne, beige, rust and a darker beige . . . a taffeta top and the skirt—oh, the skirt was a dream come true: layers and layers of short, net ruffles so that it stood out majestically. And it was the popular short, ballerina length.

"Perhaps you'd like to look at other dresses. We have quite a nice selection in the back. Many are . . . reasonably priced," she suggested.

"No, that's my dress. I'll try it on."

She wasn't smiling when she announced, "It's over sixty dollars!"

Over sixty dollars! So much more than Mama and I had talked about. That was an enormous price back in 1957. But I was already in a relationship with the dress. I reached out and lightly touched a stiff net ruffle. "May I use your phone?"

"Local call?" She looked even more grim.

"No. I'll reverse the charge."

"Hello, Mama!" I'd reached her at work in Elberton. "I found the dress. But, Mama, it's . . . over sixty dollars!"

A pause. By standing on tiptoe I could still see the dress from the telephone.

"Marion, I want you to get the dress. You'll always remember this weekend. It's going to be . . . special."

"Mama, the saleslady thinks I should look at cheaper dresses," I said, lowering my voice.

"Let me speak to her, please."

I held the phone out to the small, unsmiling woman with her arms folded stiffly about her waist. "My mama wants to talk to you." She pulled off an enormous earring and put the phone to her ear.

"Yes. Yes! Of course. Certainly, ma'am." The woman's entire countenance and voice changed. She was smiling. She hung the phone up and said in a new, soft voice, "Come right this way, Miss Bond. I'll help you into the dress. Your mother wants you to have long gloves. She's absolutely right, of course. The dress will be perfect with your auburn hair, dear."

> "Yes. Yes! Of course. Certainly, ma'am." The woman's entire countenance and voice changed.

Even barefoot, I knew at last how Cinderella felt. It was all I could manage not to waltz over the plush carpet. Several customers stopped and smiled. The saleslady stood with her hands clasped together, almost as though she were praying. Then she brought long ivory gloves that came up to my elbows. Mama had arranged for me to charge it all.

The next weekend I took the new dress home to Elberton for Mama to see. She loved it as much as I did. Then I returned to Atlanta to my job. Only one more week and my new dress and I would be on the Silver Comet.

I was back in my apartment in Atlanta when Mama called. When I heard her say, "Oh, Marion," I knew instantly. I could see the dress hanging on the back of her bedroom door in its clear zipped bag. How could I have forgotten it? I was to board the Silver Comet in Atlanta on Friday and ride overnight to Virginia.

My heart tumbled to my feet. I had to work all week. So did Mama. How would I get my Cinderella dress for the ball?

"I'll stop the train, Marion," Mama said. She sounded confident. But how? The Silver Comet usually whizzed by my little hometown nightly, blowing its horn frantically at the crossing. "Don't worry," Mama urged me once again.

But I did worry—all week. Suppose we just sped through Elberton? That's what the train did when no one got on or off. How could I go to the big dance without my once-in-a-lifetime dress?

Then it was Friday. I was on the train speeding toward Elberton. Worrisome thoughts seemed to speed through my mind, over and over. After a while in the late afternoon sun I began to see sweetly familiar landmarks. My heart thumped loudly. On the outskirts of town I recognized houses. And the giant oak tree. Then there were the granite sheds. They didn't look like much—tin buildings that appeared to be hurriedly thrown together, but beautiful cemetery markers were skillfully created in those sheds. The granite—a rough marblelike rock—lay buried underneath many parts of Elberton. We were known as the Granite Center of the South. My heart suddenly felt like granite, heavy and cold. We were getting close to the train station. Can Mama really do it?

I sat on the very edge of my seat, biting my lip, trying to decide if the train was slowing down. Was it? Or was it simply my deep longing? The scenes outside didn't seem to be passing by as rapidly. It was slowing down! Then the train screeched to a glorious halt!

I looked outside. There it was—the Elberton Depot. It had never looked so wonderful. The building was brick with a slanted roof and long windows; it resembled the miniature depots that came with train sets.

Suddenly everyone turned to stare. I did too. There was Mama! She shot me a victorious I-told-you-so smile, as though she stopped trains all the time. Mama came down the aisle like the Queen of England, holding my dress up high. The porter helped her find a place to hang it. She gave me a quick, hard hug and hurried off the impatient train. Not a word had been spoken. It was all a beautiful pantomime.

The train rumbled to life again. I pressed my face to the window and waved joyfully, gratefully as we continued on to Virginia that unforgettable evening. Mama stood waving back to me with both hands.

Now, standing there with Jamie as she tries on the dress, I tell her the story. I tell her about Mama's stopping the Silver Comet because she knew the weekend would be special. And it was. As it turned out, that weekend was the first time Jerry West and I talked of marriage.

"But Nanny," Jamie exclaims when I finish, "how did she stop the train?"

Oh, that! To tell the truth, until this moment I have never tried to find out; I've always enjoyed the mystery. Yet Jamie's question makes me wonder, so I telephone Mama.

There is a pause on the other end and I know Mama is thinking. Then she says, "Well, he's dead now; I suppose I can tell you. You see, Mr. Crisp, the depot agent at that time, was a lifelong friend of mine. So I told him about your dress and asked if he wouldn't stop the train. In small towns, Marion, people extend their friends . . . certain courtesies. You remember the verse: 'Ask, and it shall be given you; seek, and you shall find . . . ' It's true. So many times, all you have to do is ask."

Marion Bond West

House Hunters

Often newsletters and other regular mailings are good sources of humor. To help house hunters, *Have a Good Day* newsletter listed handy translations for real estate terms:

Unobstructed view: No trees.

Waiting your imaginative touch: Complete disrepair.

Handyman's dream: Owner's nightmare.

Pond site: Swamp, slough, or marsh.

Land alone worth purchase price: It had better be; the house is worthless.

House alone worth purchase price: Small lot next to tavern.

Central to everything: A very noisy area.

Easy commuting: Remote from everything.

Country kitchen: No dining room.

Charm all its own: Don't lean on the old porch railing.

All services available: Nothing hooked up.

Secluded: No road in.

On paved road: House is ten feet from busy highway.

Needs finishing touches: Needs roof.

Rustic appeal: Outdoor plumbing.

Rusty Wright and Linda Raney Wright

MISS FANNY ROLLINS OF PEAR ORCHARD, U.S.A.

Back where I'm from, there's a small town known as Pear Orchard. Actually, there's nothing much to Pear Orchard; it's just an ordinary little town. It's located somewhere between El Paso and Texarkana. The Chamber of Commerce down there has a motto: Pear Orchard, U.S.A.—the biggest little town in the country.

Some people might say, "Well, it's a typical town of the Silent Majority." It might be typical of the majority, but there ain't nothing silent about it. The first time I ever visited the place, I found a new friend while looking for a rocking chair. The local furniture store clerk told me they didn't stock rockers anymore but said if I would drive out to see Miss Fanny Rollins, she might have one that she had no more use for.

When I arrived at her mailbox, I could see a long, oleander-bordered walkway leading up to the front porch of a country farm home. A woman was sitting in a porch swing taking up room for four people. That capacious soul was spread all over the swing, her arms resting on her ample bosom, which went all the way around to her backbone, just like a hen fixing to fly off a low roof. I said, "How do, ma'am. I'm looking for Miss Fanny Rollins."

"Heh, heh. Well, honey," she said, "you'd better get an eye doctor if you can't see her. I've been accused of a heap of things, but being invisible ain't one of them. Have a chair, sit down . . . That little rocker? . . . Yes, it is a nice one . . . No, I wouldn't be interested in selling it . . . Oh, no. It's funny you mention it, because my daughter-in-law Bertha Mae, Gervis's wife, was over here the other day asking for it. Of course, I can't set in it at all, now. It would take three of them to hold me.

"Bertha Mae's a sweet girl. And talented! Folks don't know it, but bless her heart, she can rub her stomach and pat her head and recite all the books of the Bible backwards. And stop right in the middle to whistle a spiritual. Even preachers can't do that. All her family was talented that way.

"Her oldest brother, Fred, he's one-armed. I don't know how he lost his arm, it was either in a haybaler or a car accident, but I know it was an accident. He didn't do it on purpose. He had a 1952 pickup truck and a double hernia and he could train dogs like nobody I seen. Had that old blue-tick hound named Scooter. Scooter was three-legged, and ever so often people would say, 'I wonder why God left that dog's hind leg off him?'

"God has a purpose. Most dogs, you know, have to slow down to smell around a bush. Well, Scooter scarcely had to pause. He'd do his business and be gone. Fred had him trained to carry a milk bucket. Fred, being one-armed, couldn't pack two buckets of milk at the same time, so Scooter carried the other. Wouldn't spill a drop. Fred had him trained to where he would say, 'Scooter! The wood box is empty,' and Scooter would get up, go trotting out to that woodpile on three legs, pick up a mouthful of kindling, and come drop it in the wood box.

"You know, it's a funny thing, I give Scooter a heap of credit, but not for good judgment when it comes to dynamite and wood. There was a road construction crew working out there one day and Scooter came trotting in with a stick of dynamite. Dropped it in the wood box. And Fred, absentminded-like, stuck it in the stove.

"I'll say this, it was as interesting a funeral as we ever had here. Never found nothing but Fred's left shoe, and his foot was still in it. The family went down to Cartwright's Funeral Parlor and asked for a left-foot coffin. Cartwright said they didn't stock them. Well, they argued back and forth for the longest time, and the family finally settled for buying the whole coffin. I thought it was amusing to see—a coffin big enough for a whole corpse, with just a left foot in it.

"All of that family was talented like that. Take that little old Annie Lee. Oh, that was a sweet thing. But she had a lot of tragedy. When she was about thirteen years old, she went out to the barn to milk the cows and there come up a thunderstorm. Lightning struck her right between the eyes. It soured both buckets of milk. Electricity is strange. It give that child a terrible headache. They thought at first that's all it did, but it turned out to have straightened her hair.

"Oh, bless her little old heart, she tried to get it curly again. She put it up in paper curlers and left it up for thirty-six days in a row as a trial run. She took the curlers out, run her comb through it, and it was straight as a horse's tail. Course that ain't all lightning will do to you—it flattened that child's chest. Well, honey, I ain't talking about being just flat-chested, she was ironing-board flat-chested.

"But she went to town and got her a job working at the state highway department. Saved her money and bought her a pair of foam-rubber bosoms. Oh, it changed her whole outlook on life—from the front. Annie Lee got to where she'd come to church twice on Sunday. Even started singing in the Methodist choir, and she had no more voice than a white leghorn pullet.

"It was all because of the bosoms. And she started coming to our quilting parties every Friday. We had a little old Methodist preacher named Brother Walker; he'd stand there while we quilted, hoorahing with us ladies. Annie Lee was setting at the frame behind me. Brother Walker, he was laughing and chatting, and all of a sudden his jaw went slack, sweat popped out on his brow, and his eyes rolled back in his head. I thought he was having a fainting spell. I said, 'Brother Walker, are you well?' He didn't answer me at all; he just grabbed the doorknob and went through the door mumbling, 'Oh, Lord, oh, Lord.' I turned my eyes and seen the occasion for the whole thing. Annie Lee was using that left bosom as a pincushion. She'd run that Big Number Nine needle clear through from one side to the other.

"Annie Lee kept on using those bosoms until she found Totsie Taylor and married him. But she still had a lot of tragedy, honey. Totsie was a-setting on the railroad tracks one day, just a-thinking of something, when the *Katy Flyer* came by at seven hundred miles an hour and hit him. Well, I say hit him. It exploded him. He was sitting there one minute and the next he was a puff of mist floating across the field. They estimated his remainders floated over two and a half acres. The family leased about four acres for the funeral, just to be safe. The pallbearers all had a turn at the plow. Brother Culpepper came from Liberty Hill and said it was the biggest funeral he ever preached. Acreage-wise.

"Brother Culpepper always knowed the right thing to say. You know, he preached Papa's funeral. Papa passed away sitting in that little rocker that you're in right now. He had such a quiet passing, I didn't know he was gone, to tell the truth. One afternoon, I was shelling black-eyed peas in my lap. Just a-chatting and a-talking to him and he'd grunt every once in a while. After a while, I didn't notice him a-grunting. I looked up, and he was gone. No death rattle, no struggle. His head just dropped forward. Drop your head forward, honey . . . Now let it hang down . . . There, just like that. I've always said I ain't no scientist, but if that had been a straight chair, Papa would have come out of it and I would have knowed he was dead. Straight chair won't hold a corpse. But Papa's body just rocked back in that little rocker. That's the reason, honey, I wouldn't sell it for anything in the world. It's got sentimental value to it."

John Henry Faulk

Classified Ads

I find some amazing things in the newspapers. These are actual classified ads:

From the Saginaw, Michigan, *News:* For Sale—Eight puppies from a German Shepherd and an Alaskan Hussy.

From the Roanoke, Illinois, *Review:* Hope chest—brand-new, half-price, long story.

From the help wanted ads in a Michigan paper: Adult or mature teenager to baby-sit. One dollar an hour—plus fridge benefits.

From the Los Altos, California, *Town Crier:* Lost: Gray and white female cat. Answers to electric can opener.

Midwestern newspaper ad: Idaho bachelor wants wife. Must be interested in farming and own tractor. Please enclose picture of tractor.

From *The New York Times:* Young man, Democrat, would like to meet young lady, Republican. Object: third party.

Notice to the person or persons who took the large pumpkin on Highway 87 near Southridge Storage: please return the pumpkin and be checked. Pumpkin may be radioactive. All other plants in vicinity are dead.

Tired of working for only $9.75 per hour? We offer profit sharing and flexible hours. Starting pay: $7–$9 per hour.

Help Wanted: Busy lawyer seeks alert young woman to serve as deceptionist.

For Rent: One-bedroom apt. Adults, no pets. Well, maybe a cat.

Help Wanted: Saleslady for cosmetic counter in department store. Must like people part or full time.

Help Wanted: Secretary wants job; no bad habits; willing to learn.

From a display ad for an automotive dealership in Cleveland, Tennessee: "Why go anywhere else and get cheated when you can come here!"

The Orange Street Food Farm ran an ad in the Missoula, Montana, *Missoulian* for "Golden, Ripe, Boneless Bananas, 39 cents a pound."

Help Wanted: From the York, Pennsylvania, *Daily Record:* Attention: good hours, excellent pay, fun place to work, paid training, mean boss. Oh well, four out of five isn't bad.

Main Street Mirth

FOR SALE:

1 man, 7 woman hot tub—$850/offer.

Snow blower . . . only used on snowy days.

Free puppies . . . part German Shepherd—part dog.

2 wire mesh butchering gloves: 1 5-finger, 1 3-finger, pair: $15.

'83 Toyota hunchback—$2,000.

Star Wars job of the hut—$15.

Free puppies: ½ Cocker Spaniel—½ sneaky neighbor's dog.

Free Yorkshire Terrier. 8 years old. Unpleasant little dog.

German Shepherd. 85 lbs. Neutered. Speaks German. Free.

Free 1 can of pork and beans with purchase of 3 bedroom 2 bath home.

For Sale: Lee Majors (6 Million Dollar Man)—$50.

Nordic Track $300 hardly used. Call Chubbie.

Shakespeare's Pizza—free chopsticks.

Hummels—largest selection ever. If it's in stock, we have it!

Harrisburg postal employees gun club.

Georgia peaches—California grown—89 cents lb.

Nice parachute: never opened—used once—slightly stained.

Free: farm kittens. Ready to eat.

American flag—60 stars—pole included $100.

Exercise equipment: queen size mattress and box springs—$175.

Joining nudist colony! Must sell washer and dryer $300.

Ground beast: 99 cents lb.

Open House—Body Shapers Toning Salon—free coffee and donuts.

Fully cooked boneless smoked man—$2.09 lb.

Puppies for sale. Mother registered AKC St. Bernard. Father, a VERY REMARKABLE beagle.

100-year-old brass bed. Perfect for antique lovers.

Amana washer $100. Owned by clean bachelor who seldom washed.

Complete set of *Encyclopedia Britannica*. 45 volumes. Excellent condition. $1,000.00 or best offer. No longer needed. Got married last weekend. Wife knows everything.

Monster! John Deere, 38′, front-end, snow blower. Hurls snow from your drive well into neighbor's property. (I did, he got mad, that's why I'm selling.)

We put up the loot; daughter won't toot. First $175 takes the flute.

Free Tasmanian devil. Currently disguised as small puppy. Good watchdog.

Van—'94 Dodge Grand Caravan. One owner, lady driver, loaded.

Fiberglass boat, 2 sets of sails & spinnaker, trailer. Must sell, crew pregnant.

Lowell D. Streiker

6

Programs, Preachers, PTA, and Politics

Is there anything more entertaining than local programs and events? Who's running for what, what programs they're promoting, and what happened at this month's PTA meeting keep a town—large or small—loathing or laughing.

A FLAMING SPEECH

News travels fast in our small town, and when word got out that I had coauthored a book about worms—*Worms in My Tea*—my status immediately grew. As a matter of fact, I found myself proudly introduced in public places as "the author with worms." Another friend came up with a promotion ploy—suggesting Mother and I wear buttons that read "Ask us about our worms."

With that sort of interest, of course, invitations to speak began to pour in. Well, perhaps *trickle* might be a more accurate word for it. (Okay, so I dropped a hint over the phone to the Ladies' Committee Chairwoman from my church that I just might be available to speak at our annual Ladies' Class Christmas Coffee.)

When I arrived at the home where the coffee was to take place, it looked like it belonged to Martha Stewart on one of her better Christmases. Elegant it was, with a roaring fire in the huge stone fireplace, luxurious furniture covered in rich tapestries, and the entire house accented with holly, ivy, lace, candles, flowers—the works.

By a great miracle I had arrived early, and I soon saw that the hostesses were having trouble with the spout of the gorgeous silver coffee urn. It would not stop dripping. There it stood in the middle of the white damask cloth, nicely lit by a votive candle on either side, its spout creating a puddle in a hastily placed crystal punch cup. I couldn't help thinking that perhaps the Spirit had prompted me to arrive early because He had foreseen my skills would be needed. (Readers of *Worms in My Tea* will already know that I have become somewhat of an expert on leaking things—appliances, car radiators, commodes, sewers. Why wouldn't these skills transfer to an elegant silver coffee urn?)

I jiggled the spout in a more professional manner than the hostess had been jiggling it, and when the puddle continued to grow, I bent low and tried to peer up the spout itself. Clearly I was onto something. A most peculiar odor became apparent—it was followed by a puff of smoke wafting before my eyes. Suddenly the hostesses sprang at me from all directions, beating me about the head and shoulders with towels and tossing cups of water in my general direction. When I realized I had managed to ignite my own hair with the votive candles beside the urn, I did exactly what I had taught my first-graders to do in our "Safety First" course: I stopped, dropped, and rolled all the way to an easy chair where the hostesses insisted I stay until it was time for me to speak.

"We don't want anything else to happen, Becky," they assured me. I was touched by their concern.

My topic for the morning was "Taking Time to Wonder as You Wander Through the Season," and I'm sure the ladies were indeed wondering why the hostess had included fragrance of singed hair in the potpourri on her tables. (Considering the elegance of the rest of her decorations, I expect we may have seen the evolution of an entirely new Christmas fragrance. I watch for it every year. It transports one almost immediately to a stable.)

I had planned to end my talk with a moving quote about the love of a father for his young son. At this tender, emotion-charged moment, the Sterno heater on the buffet table suddenly ignited, shooting flames about two feet into the air. It created quite a stir, but our Christmas Coffee Women's Volunteer Fire Department leaped into action, beating the flames with dish towels, trying to subdue the inferno with crystal cups full of punch and coffee, and finally extinguishing the persistent flames with an inverted fondue pot.

When the hostesses looked in my direction, I was thankful I had been standing at least three yards from the table during the entire event.

Afterward I went straight home, called my mother, gave her all the details of my first speech, and told her how we might need to bring portable fire extinguishers to any future events we might do together. She laughed, I laughed, and then in the background, I could hear my father asking for details. "So, how'd Becky do?"

Though her voice was a bit muffled, I could hear her praise me as only a truly creative mother can: "Honey, she was on fire. The audience simply melted in her hair . . . uh . . . I mean hands."

Becky Freeman

A traffic safety consultant often gave talks on accident prevention. One night after he spoke to a PTA group, the program chairperson thanked him profusely and gave him a check for $50.

"Giving these presentations is a part of my job," the consultant said. "Could I donate the money to one of your causes?"

"That would be wonderful!" the chairperson said.

"I know just the program that needs it the most. We're trying to raise money so we can afford better speakers."

Jim Kraus

• •

Our town was small but we got two things we're very proud of. Night and day. If you have a year to live, move there—it'll seem like a lifetime.

George "Goober" Lindsey

• •

OUTDOOR NEWSPAPER

Some little burgs are worth stopping in just because they have a good sense of humor. I have a great fondness for such places. The citizens of these towns refuse to take themselves very seriously, with the result that they have a dandy lot of fun just getting up in the morning and walking around town and being alive. I've often tried without any success to figure out why it is that some towns have fun all the time while others of the same size and similar background sit around all long-faced, talking about their ancestors and how much better things were in the old days.

In Wharton County there's a town called Louise. Has 882

citizens. Even the Chamber of Commerce of Louise has a sense of humor. This is pretty astonishing, because most Chambers of Commerce in towns of that size view themselves with an awesome seriousness.

Ralph Stockton, who is just a guy you meet when you go to Louise, explained to me with a straight face, "When we organized a Chamber of Commerce we wanted to put up a clean front, so we elected Baldy Crowell president because he's the only man in town who takes a bath and shaves every morning. Besides, he's got the only air-conditioned office in town and it makes a good place to meet. Paul Sablatura, our county commissioner, introduces Baldy at the Chamber-of-Commerce meetings as the past, present, and future president, and for a slogan we adopted 'Leave It to Baldy.'"

This slogan is printed in boldface type in the local telephone directory and would be expensive to change if anybody else got Crowell's position, so he seems in office to stay. But if Louise had a city charter and a local government, which it doesn't, the mayor would be Sablatura. As county commissioner, he keeps all the streets paved and the vacant lots mowed, and nobody has to pay city taxes for these services. But in addition to that, Sablatura is a good musician and entertainer, and is so handy to have around at special occasions like celebrations. He works without any pay, just the same as Crowell does. Crowell, along with his brother Bo, is a driller of water wells, and both of them distribute business cards that say, "Help Stamp Out Windmills."

There's always something a little different, amusing, or interesting or offbeat, going on around Louise that makes life interesting there. Small things, sometimes, that you may discover just by walking into Raymond Hillyer's Grocery Store. The difference I found between going into Hillyer's and going into a grocery store in the city was that at the check-out stand Mrs. Lucille Rutledge had a fruit jar sitting by the cash register with a big green worm in it. This was being displayed for the amazement of the customers. It was a beautiful worm. He had spots all over him in various brilliant colors—yellow, green, blue, orange. You wouldn't find a prettier worm anywhere, and in Louise it seemed right and proper that it be exhibited at the grocer's.

Ralph Stockton always claimed that, since Louise is not big enough to afford a full-time town drunk, various of the men around town take turns filling the role, so the job won't be too hard on any one fellow's constitution. Well, of course you know that isn't true, just the same as it's not true that M. W. (Baldy) Crowell is the only man in town that shaves every morning. All the same, I find it refreshing in contrast to the overabundance of little towns that are sick with pride and self-importance and that might, if anybody suggested it, issue a straight-faced news release announcing that the town doesn't have a single drunk and that all the men shave and bathe every day.

Visitors to Louise are generally taken over to the mill and presented with a sack of brown rice. The town is located in the heart of the Texas rice belt, and Ralph Stockton maintains that all its citizens eat this unpolished rice. "That's how it's eaten over in China," Stockton says, "where the men live to be a hundred and become fathers every year." Stockton has not been able to explain why it is, then, that Louise has a population of no more than 882.

Among the notable things at Louise is its newspaper, which is the biggest in Texas, and maybe in the world. That is, if you judge it by page size and not circulation. A page of this newspaper measures eight by sixteen feet, and if that sounds to you like a billboard, you are right. This outdoor newspaper stands beside a small drive-in grocery on U.S. 59. The editor is Tillie Roome, who works in the grocery store. When she hears a piece of news, she runs out to the billboard with a piece of chalk and writes it up. Anybody that wants to catch up on the news, then, just drives by the grocery store and reads it, without even getting out of the car.

Tillie Roome has a press card issued by the Texas Department of Public Safety to prove she is a newspaper editor. The news she deals in includes such items as who is in the hospital and who has had a baby, and who is valedictorian at the high school, and other school and church announcements. If there's no fresh news, the editor just changes the date and lets the same news run that ran the day before. There is no charge for advertising, and you will find offered in the classified section a Toulouse goose and twelve goslings and similar bargains.

Baldy Crowell, in addition to being chamber-of-commerce president is fishing editor of the outdoor newspaper. In one edition I read, Crowell had reported that the trout were biting live shrimp at Half Moon Reef in Matagorda Bay, a few miles south on the coast. Some fisherman, apparently having taken Baldy's advice, had returned empty-creeled to scrawl a comment alongside Crowell's report, indicating it wasn't worth the chalk it took to write it.

Now that is the beautiful thing about having an outdoor newspaper. Any reader that doesn't agree with what he reads can just come along and write in a rebuttal.

Leon Hale

••

Human nature cannot be studied in cities except at a disadvantage—a village is the place. There you can know your man inside and out—in a city you but know his crust; and his crust is usually a lie.

Mark Twain

••

THE FAMILY CIRCUS　　　　　**By Bil Keane**

"They're not trying on clothes. They're voting."

YOU ARE HERE

My husband, David, and I have just worked out at our neighborhood YMCA, and I am waiting for him near the men's dressing room. I have no less than a jillion things to do before the day is over, and the thought of the long day ahead fills my insides with a familiar panic. I pace up and down the hall, and when I look up, I find myself staring at a sign posted on the wall. "You are here," it says. A red arrow points to a certain location marked with an X on the building's blueprint.

I am still standing there looking at the sign when David comes. "This is crazy," I say to him, "but I feel so reassured knowing exactly where I am in this busy day." David laughs, puts his arm around my shoulder, and off we go.

Later, I am working at my computer when the buzzer on the dryer sounds. On my way to remove David's shirts, I smell the chicken dish cooking in the kitchen and change my direction to check on it. Passing the dining room, I notice that I haven't yet set the table for tonight's guests. A moment of cold fear falls over me. *Can I really handle all of this?* Then I remember the sign. "You are here," I remind myself as I open the oven door. The casserole is fine.

After I have the shirts on hangers, I return to my desk and jot down all the things I need to accomplish before the day ends, numbering them by priority. "You are here," I say out loud as I draw a red arrow to number one on the blueprint of my day.

Realizing that today actually can be managed, one task at a time, I stop and smile. "I am here," I say to God, "and You are here. Let's turn this into a good, productive day together." And we do!

Pam Kidd

•••

The local veterinarian in a small town in Maine was treating a vacationer's dog that had had an unfortunate encounter with a porcupine.

After prying, pulling, cutting, and stitching, he returned the dog to its owner.

"How much will that be?" the out-of-towner asked.

"A hundred dollars, Ma'am," the vet answered.

"Why that's simply outrageous!" she stormed. "You're always trying to overcharge nonresidents. What do you do in the winter, when we're not here to be gypped?"

"Raise porcupines, ma'am."

Jim Kraus

•••

CAPPUCCINO COWBOYS

I am constantly amazed and amused by this life I'm now leading—so far removed from the one I once knew.

A few years ago, I drove up to the high school with my 13-year-old daughter, Rachel. I asked her to run over and give a sports drink to her older brother, Zeke, who was about to begin an after-school session of football practice. She soon returned, breathlessly diving into the front seat.

"So, Rachel, that was fast," I commented. "Did you give Zeke the Gatorade?"

"No," she responded calmly, "I gave it to Goof."

"Pardon me?"

"I gave it to Goof Fry and told him to give it to Zeke."

"Hold it. Are you telling me there is a child who goes by the name of 'Goof' at your school?"

"Yep. It's what everyone calls him."

"Even the teachers?"

"Mo-*ther*, yes! Everybody calls him that—the teachers, his parents, the whole school. Nobody ever thinks about it being strange or anything. He's Ida Lou's brother."

Scratching my head, I said, "So let me get this straight. There are a pair of siblings in your school named Goof and Ida Lou Fry."

"Yes."

I grinned. Rachel, eyeing me suspiciously, asked, "What are you smiling about?"

"Oh," I replied, "I just love country life, that's all."

On our way home, Rachel and I stopped off at the local grocery store to pick up a couple of hot barbeque sandwiches and some cold Dr. Peppers. There, lying on the counter was a flyer from the taxidermist next door. "This is too good," I said aloud as I scanned the paper. Here, in brief, are the actual contents of the flyer.

Varmint Tournament
Bobcats 100 points
Coyotes 50 points
Big cat and big coyote judged by weight, not by length.
All animals entered in contest will be checked thoroughly
to verify fresh kills.
Let's keep this an honest and fun event.

How would one go about cheating in a varmint contest? I wondered. What—do some unscrupulous hunters try to fluff up road kill and pass it off as a freshly killed varmint?

Becky Freeman

•••

In the midst of a busy morning, the country agricultural agent got a call from a woman who said she was starting a chicken farm and wanted to know how long she should leave the rooster with the hens.

"Just a minute," said the agent, who was busy talking on another phone.

"Thank you very much," said the woman and hung up.

Tal D. Bonham

•••

Aphorisms for Our Time

If at first you don't succeed, skydiving is not for you.

Money can't buy happiness. But it sure makes misery easier to live with.

Vital papers will demonstrate their vitality by moving from where you left them to where you can't find them.

Always remember to pillage before you burn.

The trouble with doing something right the first time is that nobody appreciates how difficult it was.

Ray's Law: You can't fall off the floor.

Paranoids are people too; they have their own problems. It's easy to criticize, but if everybody hated you, you'd be paranoid too.

Eagles may soar, but weasels aren't sucked into jet engines.

Jim Kraus

- - -

When the power failed at the elementary school, the cook couldn't serve a hot meal in the cafeteria, so at the last minute she whipped up huge stacks of peanut butter and jelly sandwiches. As one little boy filled his plate, he said, "It's about time. Finally, a home-cooked meal."
Lowell D. Streiker

- - -

TRUCK FOR ALL SEASONS

For months I had looked forward to that spring Saturday. David Harden, a traveling folk artist I'd met through my sideline of home decorating, was coming to paint scenes on our kitchen cabinets. I paused at the window and made a mental list of paintings for him—a profusion of spring cro-

Programs, Preachers, PTA, and Politics 117

cuses, a brilliant October pumpkin festival, ice skaters at the old mill pond.

As I sipped tea, my husband, Mark, slammed the door, jarring me back to reality. He wiped his grease-stained hands on my new kitchen towel and hugged my shoulder with a strong arm. Gulping a swig of muddy black coffee six hours old, Mark pointed his grungy thermal mug toward our picket fenced courtyard. "Will you have a look at that?" he crowed. "Over by the arbor. A volunteer tomato plant! I just staked it." Sure enough, center stage between my climbing pink roses and my herb garden was a spindly tomato plant, staked with the stub of a broken truck axle.

Just what I needed—a reminder of Mark's confounded ancient truck. I despised that eyesore with all of its accessories. The truck made so many noises traveling at 35 miles an hour, you couldn't even hear the radio. Each noise, Mark insisted, served as a diagnostic indicator known only to him. And there was always something in need of repair. Mark often got a hankering to tinker on it in the wee hours of the morning. With running lights lining the cab, it glowed like a carnival in the dark. I felt we were the laughingstock of our neighborhood.

"Why don't we buy a new truck?" I'd often suggested. Mark always answered, "No, I just can't see dropping a ton of gravel or a load of firewood in the bed of a new truck. This one's fine. I can kick back and relax with my old truck. Why, even if we were millionaires, I'd have to think twice about letting it go."

I remembered how the week before, I'd climbed over dirty rags, coffee mugs, quarts of motor oil, a toolbox, and a baying beagle to accompany Mark to the auto store. I'd cringed in embarrassment at a McDonald's drive-through when Mark noisily obliged two kids who pumped their arms up and down, signaling him to blow his horn. Words from the third chapter of Ecclesiastes had flashed through my mind: "There is a time for everything . . . a time to be silent and a time to speak." When it came to his prized truck, my husband forgot about everything, especially silence. Mark had cackled out the window to the grinning boys, "I salvaged this jewel of a horn from a big ol' tractor trailer down at the junkyard."

Now Mark asked, "Where's our artist? I want him to paint our new tomato plant on these cabinets. You did give him our phone—"

"Of course," I snapped. "He can't miss this place. I gave him the same directions I give everyone else: Look for the red Sanford and Son truck in the driveway."

When David at long last arrived, he inquired about our favorite memories. The cabinet doors became his canvas as he and Mark swapped stories. David painted a red schoolhouse from Mark's childhood, a cobblestoned herb garden for me, dogs we had loved, a carefree young couple sleigh riding. But then I saw Mark's truck marring the perfection of a summer-day scene beside bins of vegetables labeled "Messner's Produce Stand."

"Good grief," I cried, "I never bargained for that dratted truck and those vegetables. Next thing I know, Mark will be farming and peddling produce door-to-door."

"Well," David answered with a grin, "these things are always open to change. Do you think we should move the truck to fall? It would work well with a hayride scene. Or how about winter, bringing in a load of firewood? I see this as a truck for all seasons."

In a quiet but firm voice I said, "I don't want it in spring. I don't want it in summer. I don't want it in fall. And I don't want it in winter. The truck doesn't belong in the picture at all. Not in the background. Definitely not in the foreground. It's a truck for no season."

David looked stricken. "You should have seen the happy look on Mark's face when he saw his truck in the scene," he answered.

I didn't have time to argue. In less than an hour I was scheduled to decorate a bedroom at a designers' showcase in a neighboring town. Mark had offered to help me move the furnishings with his truck, and he happily revved the engine as we headed out the drive.

"Promise you won't embarrass me," I pleaded. "And no air horns today!"

Once at the showcase home, Mark and I navigated the cumbersome bedroom suite and boxes of accessories up the elegant staircase. "While you get the room situated, I'll have some coffee outside," he said. "Holler when you need the rest of the furniture."

Moments later I heard whispering and laughter in the next room. "Just look out there behind that old truck," a lady exclaimed. "There's a guy sitting in a chair by a wicker table."

Oh, no, I thought. I tiptoed toward their voices, hanging on every word.

"Now he has the right idea," said another woman. "Wouldn't it be wonderful to be like that—so content and at ease with yourself?"

"That man must have some wife," a guy piped up. "Mine makes me lock my '59 Chevy in the garage. Says it embarrasses her to death."

I mustered the courage to join the group of designers and looked out the second-story window. There was Mark having coffee in his own cozy little "room" he'd arranged in the street next to his beloved truck.

Suddenly, I was laughing. I felt a surge of warmth for Mark and a startling new kinship with the truck. I had to admit, it did have its fine points. Always there in weather fair or foul—dependable and unpretentious—just like Mark.

Later, as we pulled away, I admitted, "I guess I have been a little unreasonable about this truck. Everyone's got something dear to him that others don't always understand." The words from Ecclesiastes once again flashed through my mind: "There is a time for everything . . . a time to be silent and a time to speak."

I couldn't resist the urge to reach over and give a blast on the air horn. The truck rang with the noise of laughter as we headed home.

Roberta Messner

INCIDENT ON HAZEL STREET

"As the snow continues to develop on my roof and the fire dims in my basement," Lou joked, "I am noticing more signs of the aging process."

Lou's cousin Wanda had been visiting the church where Lou is the pastor. He had been out of touch with her and her family through the years, so he admitted he didn't know much about her. The visitor's card she signed revealed that she lived at 501 Hazel Street. "I knew she was divorced and had resumed using her maiden name, which is the same as mine—Jones," he added.

As Lou drove down Hazel Street, he spotted a house that he was certain was Wanda's. "I parked the car, walked to the door, and rang the bell," said Lou. "A rather husky gentleman in an unbuttoned, khaki-colored shirt greeted me. I didn't know if he was a boyfriend, a neighbor, or a new husband!"

Lou introduced himself and said he was from the Saints Rest Missionary Baptist Church. "I'm stopping by today to say hello to Wanda. She's been visiting our church lately."

"Hello there," the man replied. "I'm Buck Bender. Come on in! Wanda isn't here today. She's gone to Denton to see the kids!"

Lou kept the tone light and friendly. "Well, Wanda and I are distant cousins," he said, smiling.

"Really? What side of the family?" asked Buck.

"The Jones side."

"Jones?" Buck looked puzzled. "My wife wasn't a Jones. She was a McDonald! But you've got the first name right. It's Wanda."

Suddenly Lou was a bit suspicious. "Is this address 501 Hazel Street?" he asked, feeling a bit embarrassed.

"No," said Buck. "It's 507. The little curly-q broke off the top of the number seven, so now it looks like a one."

Lou backed out the doorway and extended his hand. "Well, it's been real good visiting with you, Buck! And give my regards to Wanda—even if she's someone else's cousin!"

Karen O' Connor

© www.CartoonStock.com

•••

School days are the happiest days of your life— providing, of course, your youngsters are old enough to go.

Paul Selden

•••

THE 2-FOR-1 HAIRCUT

A few months ago we loaded up Jedd's Geo GL (which we think stands for Gullible Losers) and headed for our sister church up in North Dakota, the Church of the Frozen Tundra. This isn't its real name, of course, but we gave it this moniker after our first couple of visits there because (1) North Dakota has tundra, and (2) much of said tundra is frozen (as are many other things in North Dakota).

We always look forward to visiting COFT and speaking to the congregation there. They seem to like us, probably because they have to put up with us only once or twice a year. Also, North Dakota is cool. Its capital is Bismarck, making it the only state in the Union with a capital named after a pastry.

As we drove, we discussed topics we might share with our brethren and sistren—and the jokes we might use. (In past visits, we found we could earn robust laughter by making fun of South Dakota.)

We pulled into a truck stop near Minot to get a snack.

As we strolled to the entrance, we looked inside the establishment, which was creatively named Al's Truck Stop, and noticed two scraggly strangers inside.

"Look at those guys," Todd commented. "Haven't they heard of that great invention, the comb?"

"I don't even know if one could pull a comb through those unruly mops," Jedd noted. "When was the last time those guys got a haircut, the Carter administration?"

"Maybe they're Nazirites," Todd offered. "Like Samson."

"I doubt it." Jedd countered. "Look at how gangly they are. They aren't strong like Samson. Delilah could whup the both of them."

"You're probably right," Todd said. "Hey, look, Jedd, one of those scrawny dudes has a Broncos jacket just like yours."

"And one of them is wearing tired old gray Kmart sweats like yours."

That's when it hit us like a big North Dakota snowball. We had met the ragamuffins, and they were us (or is it "we were they"?). We were seeing our own unkempt reflections in the truck-stop window.

"Does our hair really look that bad?" Jedd asked rhetorically.

"I'm afraid so. Truck-stop windows don't lie."

At this point we did some mental retracing and deduced that we hadn't received haircuts in about four months, when we were scheduled to be on a local TV show. (We ended up getting bumped in favor of a guy who bought a half-eaten sandwich on eBay for six hundred dollars. The other half of the sandwich had been eaten by Celine Dion, or maybe it was Deion Sanders, or perhaps Dionne Warwick. It could have been Dion of Dion & the Belmonts. In any case, the discarded food of any of those celebrities was apparently more interesting than the Brothers Hafer.)

Anyway, our heads now looked like mop tops. And not fashionable mop tops like those of the Beatles. Ours were more like stringy, unruly mops that are used to clean prison rest rooms. We knew we could not face the members of our sister church like this. It would be a poor way to represent our home church. It would show a lack of moral character. Besides, the North Dakota teens would make fun of us.

As we entered downtown Minot we strained our eyes, looking for someplace that would bring order to the chaos atop our heads—for under ten bucks, if possible. We saw a couple of high-end salons, Shear Excellence and some other fancy-looking French-looking place called Tressed to Kill (or maybe it was Turn Your Head and Coif). We knew these businesses were for people beyond our social strata and income level. (You have to beware anytime you see a hair salon with a sign noting FINANCING AVAILABLE.)

We were growing desperate when we saw Kustom Kutz. We smiled at each other. Places that don't know how to spell are typically quite economical. Beyond economical, in this case. As we pulled into the KK parking lot, we saw a hand-lettered sign in the window. It read, WEEKEND SPECIAL: 2-FOR-1-HAIRCUTZ! Twenty-two minutes later, we walked through piles of our own hair to the Kustom Kutz exit, feeling lighter in spirit and lighter in the head, if you know what we mean.

However, as we headed to our car, we began to eye each other suspiciously. All this suspicious eyeing provoked the following exchange:

Todd: "Is something wrong?"
Jedd: "In what way?"
Todd: "Well, you are looking at me funny."
Jedd: "I was just looking at you that way because you are looking at *me* funny."
Todd: "Yeah . . ."
Jedd: "So, why are you doing that?"
Todd: "You first. Why are you looking at me?"
Jedd: "It's just that . . ."
Todd: "Yes?"
Jedd: "Dude, you look like a doofus."
Todd: "I'm just the way God made me, bro. And God doesn't make junk."
Jedd: "That's not what I mean. I mean your hair. Your haircut makes you look like a doofus."
Todd: "Well, so does yours!"
Jedd: "Oh, that's great! Get all defensive, why don't you? You're the older brother. You're supposed to be the mature one."
Todd: "No, I'm not being defensive. You do indeed have a problem with your hair. It looks like somebody turned a hungry badger loose on your head."
Jedd: "Are you serious? That is the same thing I was thinking about you! Only I was going to say enraged ferret instead of hungry badger."
Todd: "Well, six of one . . ."

Jedd: "Didn't you notice how your Kustom Kutz stylist was mangling your hair? Didn't you look in the mirror?"
Todd: "Well, no. I was too busy watching your Kustom Kutz stylist do a weed-whacker number on you. Besides, your lady looked like Alice from *The Brady Bunch*. So I was kinda distracted by that. But hey, why weren't you minding *your* appearance?"
Jedd: "For the same reason as yours. Only your stylist looked like Sam the butcher from *The Brady Bunch*."
Todd: "She did?"
Jedd: "She did indeed."

We reached our car, we studied our reflections in its window and we panicked. Then we looked at our watches and panicked even more. We had precisely twenty-eight minutes before we were due to entertain and edify a church auditorium full of eager North Dakotans.

Now, you might think that a couple of funny-boys could squeeze gallons of laughter out of a bad-haircut saga like this. But these haircuts weren't bad-funny. They were bad-ghastly. They were prison-camp bad and Pauly Shore unfunny.

We knew that we could not face the believers of COFT in this state. So, following the urging of that wise man Carrot Top, we dialed down the center of a pay phone and called our friend G-Dawg in Los Angeles. He's in the entertainment industry, he's cool, he's unflappable, and he's one of the few people in the country who will accept a collect call from the Brothers Hafer.

We explained our dilemma, both yakking into the phone at the same time. After we finished kvetching, he paused a few moments. Then, in a soothing, measured tone, he said, "Dudes, I have the solution. All you have to do is shave your heads."

We protested furiously. We told G-Dawg we would feel naked without our hair. We told him we feared that if we relinquished our locks, they might never grow back. We told him it would be a hot winter in North Dakota before we would ever shave our heads.

He let us vent. Then he said, "I understand your reservations. But shaved heads are in. Look at Michael Jordan. Look at Bruce Willis. Look at Charles Barkley. Look at Sinead O'Conner."

"Sinead O'Connor?!" we screamed in unison.

"Okay, okay," G-Dawg said. "Don't look at her. But do look at the other guys. They look smooth. They look confident. They save money on shampoo. Power-bald, dudes—it's the look of the future."

The call ended. We knew Mr. Dawg was right. No hair at all had to be better than the hair we were sporting. Besides, the whole Jordan/Willis/Barkley thing was working on us. On the way to the drugstore to purchase a couple of heavy-duty Bic shavers, we took turns naming more cool bald icons: Savalas, Picasso, Connery, Moby (the musician, not the whale).

We zipped into a YMCA and stood before a wall of mirrors, where we proceeded to free our respective noggins of the atrocious 2-for-1 hair butchering. We smiled as we thought of our friend's wise counsel. We wondered whom we would resemble most when we were done—basketball stars or movie action heroes?

We toweled remnant patches of shaving cream off our domes and gazed eagerly at our reflections.

We looked like two scrawny sons of Uncle Fester.

Some people look cool bald. But those people have symmetrically shaped heads that have seen the light of the sun. Our heads looked like hard-boiled eggs that had been peeled, then beaten with a small ball peen hammer.

The congregation at COFT stared at us that evening with looks of shock and pity. It was especially embarrassing to be up there not only bald but with heads dotted with tiny pieces of blood-stained toilet paper.

The whole thing was excruciatingly uncomfortable, but we did get a record-size love offering.

We drove out of Minot that evening. (We didn't get the

usual invitation to stay overnight with one of the church families. We learned later that most of them were afraid we would give their children—or their pets—nightmares.) We left filled with embarrassment and despair. Embarrassment over the pasty-domed spectacles we had made of ourselves. Despair over the prospect of having to do gig after gig with our new maimed Uncle Fester look.

How long will it take for our hair to grow back? we wondered. More importantly, how long would it take for our dignity to grow back?

As we neared the North Dakota state line, God must have decided to smile on us or at least wink at us. Because on a large sign outside a gift shop/gas station, we read the words that would cover our present humiliation and protect us from the potential rogue barbarian shops we might encounter in the future. The sign proclaimed: WEEKEND SPECIAL: 2-FOR-1 BASEBALL KAPZ!

Todd and Jedd Hafer

AUNT LIZZIE

Aunt Lizzie Thornton was born in the Piney Woods near Trinity. She is eighty-six years old now and the farthest she's ever been from home is Crockett, twenty-eight miles away.

Still, she gained her measure of fame. Around Trinity she is noted as an expert snuff dipper and spitter. She used to come to town every Saturday and bring along her favorite rope-bottomed chair. She'd park that chair out front of the feed store, watch the people, dip snuff with an elm twig and spit with remarkable skill. She could drown a fly at twelve feet.

Trinity folks walking on the street always gave Aunt Lizzie a wide berth when they went by the feed store. At the end of the day she'd leave behind her a solid brown snuff-juice stain, extending from her chair in a broad arc twelve to fifteen feet in diameter.

Aunt Lizzie hasn't been into town for a long time, so I got a friend to steer me out to her house to find out why. She was at home and feeling pretty well. It was a hot afternoon and she came out on her front porch, barefoot, to do her talking. She's a little thing. Likely doesn't weight eighty-five pounds. The years have etched a thousand lines in her face and stooped her narrow shoulders, but they haven't dulled her tongue or her wits.

Now you used to hear a great deal of talk about people still hidden deep in the East Texas woods who've never been to school, never seen a train, never seen a city, never even ridden in a car. Perhaps they exist. I've not found them. Well, sure, there are a good many who've not been to school, or at least not enough to read and write. And many more who can read and write like sixty who've not seen a city.

Aunt Lizzie just never did recognize any necessity for seeing a city. Once a week she went into Trinity, which has eighteen hundred people. And then she traveled twenty-eight miles that time all the way to Crockett, which is a county seat town and has more than five thousand folks and a courthouse and a county fair, and if she saw a city it'd just be the same things only more of them. So she stayed home. Except on Saturdays.

Aunt Lizzie still has her rope-bottomed chair. She pulled it out on the porch and we had a question-and-answer session.

Does she still dip snuff?

"Yessirboss," she said, using an old country expression. And saying it just that way, without any commas or spaces between the words. The "boss" part of the expression doesn't imply that she is recognizing a better. It's just a way of giving an emphatic answer.

How long has she dipped snuff now?

"I don't know. Started when I was a little girl. Ten, maybe. Used to steal snuff from my mother."

Does she think seventy-five years of snuff dipping ever hurt her?"

"Naw."

Can she still spit good? Could she hit that washtub yonder by the chinaberry tree, twelve feet away?

"Could if I hadn't lost my teeth. Can't spit good without my teeth."

What would she do if the doctor told her to quit dipping?

"I'd have a dip when I wanted it. People are gonna have what they want, it don't matter what. I'm gonna have my snuff."

Why doesn't she go into town on Saturdays as she used to?

"The reason I don't," and Aunt Lizzie's eyes fired a little at the question, "I can't stand the sight of these women, wearin' pants and smokin' cigarettes. And I don't think women ought to vote, either."

Why shouldn't women vote?

"Because they're out of place at the polls. Women ought to stay in their place."

And where is that?

"At home."

How about women who work, in offices and stores?

"I don't think they ought to, but I guess it's none of my business."

Has Aunt Lizzie ever voted, even one time?

"Nosirboss."

Wouldn't she like to vote?

"Nosirboss."

Has she ever watched television?

"Saw one once. Didn't like it. That's what's makin' these children so bad, watchin' all that stuff on television."

Is Aunt Lizzie aware that men are now getting ready to fly into space and land on the moon?

"I've heard about it."

What does she think of it?

"They oughtn't to do it. That's God's moon. God put that moon there."

Does she think men will ever land on the moon?

"Naw. There's a man up there already, burnin' brush."

There's a man on the moon burning brush? How does she know that?

"Well, I can see him."

Is that what makes the moon shine, the brush burning?

"Yes."

Is that a real man up there on the moon?

"Well, I don't know. I haven't been up there to see."

Aunt Lizzie thought that was a good joke and ducked her head and laughed.

But does she believe it's a real man?

"Well, it looks like a real man."

Wouldn't Aunt Lizzie like to travel? See the ocean, go to Houston, fly in an airplane?

"Nosirboss."

Does she have any particular ambition? Anything she'd especially like to do that she's never done?

"Nosirboss. I just wanta keep on doin' just what Ima doin'."

I drove away then, and Aunt Lizzie Thornton went back to doing what she wanted to do, which was dipping snuff.

Leon Hale

DON'T QUIT

When things go wrong, as they sometimes will
When the road you're trudging seems all uphill
When the funds are low, and the debts are high
And you want to smile, but you have to sigh
When care is pressing you down a bit
Rest if you must, but don't you quit.

Success is failure turned inside out
The silver tint of clouds of doubt
And you never can tell how close you are
It may be near when it seems so far
So stick to the fight when you're hardest hit
It's when things seem worse
That you must not quit.
Author Unknown

• •

"Have any big men ever been born in this town?"
"No, just little babies."
Bob Phillips

• •

7

Neighborhood Nostalgia

From the Rockefellers to the Clampits, every neighborhood is a mixture of people and personalities. Some neighborhoods enjoy amiable peace, while others have an ongoing feud, like the Hatfields and McCoys. Either way, neighborhood shenanigans create grins and giggles.

THE NEIGHBORS NEXT DOOR

It's Saturday morning. Sunlight falls into my bedroom, drawing my eyes to the soft pastels of my wallpaper, then to the window where I can see the peak of the rooftop next door. The Coles' rooftop. My thoughts turn to the latest neighborhood news: Kristy has had her baby.

Kristy. Fifteen years old and an unwed mother. Although the Coles have lived next door for several months, I don't know them. But I have heard that Kristy's stepdad, Ron, has an eight-year-old son, Chad, from a previous marriage. And that Kristy's mom, Sue, has a teenage son, Todd, from her first marriage. Next there's two-year-old Scott, who was born to Ron and Sue. Now Kristy has made Sue a grandmother. Does that make Ron a grandfather? Or is he a step-grandparent? Or is there such a thing?

Intrigued by the relationships next door, I envision a time when Kristy is explaining who is who to Baby.

I slowly shake my head in disgust.

My husband wakes up, fluffs his pillow, and asks what's for breakfast. At the same time, I hear eight-year-old Julie bounding downstairs for morning cartoons. I roll out of bed and head for the shower. After breakfast I load the dishwasher, wipe off the counter, and work on a sewing project I'd started. Julie taps on the door.

"There's something I want to show you," she murmurs. Clearing a space, she lays down a piece of notebook paper folded in half like a greeting card. On the front is a crayoned rainbow. On the inside are large, red letters:

DEAR KRISTY, I'M HAPPY YOU HAD A BABY.
JESSICA IS A PRETTY NAME.

Hmm, I muse. *Jessica. So it's a girl* . . . Underneath is the drawing of a smiling, toothless baby and the words GOD LOVES YOU. It's signed, "Love from your next-door neighbor, Julie."

After my daughter leaves the room, I lean on the sewing table, chin in hand, and think about this. Then I go looking for my daughter.

"Don't give it to her yet," I say. "Would you like to get a little gift, too?"

"Yeah, Mom!"

We drive to K-Mart where we buy a silly yellow duck wearing a blue hat.

When we return home, Julie wraps the duck, tapes the card

on top, and we take it next door. As we wait on the porch, I'm surprised that I never noticed the pretty welcome sign. But then, I've made no effort to become acquainted with Sue at all. She has so many family members, while I've been married to the same man for over fifteen years. I'm just unable to identify with Sue's kind of life.

When Sue answers the door—that is, I think it's Sue—I am embarrassed at having to introduce myself.

"Karen, from next door. This is my daughter, Julie."

Sue, wearing her dark curly hair in a ponytail and dressed in jeans and a flannel shirt, looks quite normal. She smiles warmly and invites us in to see the baby. Kristy is on the couch, cuddling and kissing her precious bundle. Julie hands Kristy the duck and asks to hold Jessica, while I apologize.

"I'm sorry I haven't come over to meet you before now. Just busy. You know how it is."

Sue laughs and offers me a cup of coffee. I look around the room and am surprised at the cozy atmosphere. But what had I expected to see? Purple gremlins poking out of the corners, with a big sign that reads "Weird Family Lives Here"? A basket of yellow daisies rests on a side table, and on the wall above it hangs a creatively arranged collection of photos. Pictures of Sue and Ron. Kristy and Todd. Chad. Scott. And I know that a space is reserved for Jessica.

Over coffee and a crescent roll I learn more about Sue, and our woman talk turns to personal stuff—the kind where you feel so comfortable with someone you can tell her you hide candy bars in the linen closet.

"I never thought divorce would be a part of my life," Sue says. "We were married for ten years when my husband just up and left. Fell in love at the water cooler."

Ron, I learn, has been widowed for four years. "Breast cancer," Sue explains. "It was awfully hard on him." She gives a deep sigh.

"I don't know if it was the divorce, or what, but Kristy's

been a real handful lately. Now . . ." She motions to Kristy, who is fussing over the baby.

My throat begins to feel tight and funny, making it hard to swallow.

This wasn't at all what I had imagined. Suddenly I don't like myself very much.

When it's time to leave, Sue and I plan to get together again. Julie skips home across the yard, unaware that her simple, nonjudgmental act has caused a major turnabout in my judgmental heart.

After going inside, curiosity makes me reach for my Bible to look up verses with "neighbor" in them. I stop at Proverbs 11:12: "A man who lacks judgment derides his neighbor, but a man of understanding holds his tongue."

"God loves you," Julie had printed at the bottom of the card. And He does, indeed. Sue. Ron. Kristy. Todd. Chad. Scott. Jessica. Me. People.

I go to the kitchen, get out the large blue bowl, and stir up a batch of chocolate chip cookies. Sometimes it's never too late to welcome people to the neighborhood.

Karen Straud

JUNIOR

When you live in a town of one hundred people, it's usually not necessary to look out the window to check who's there before opening the front door (especially when, for most people in a small town, the front door is rarely used. Everyone knows to come in the back door, and knocking first is an optional courtesy). So when I heard the loud rap on the front door that morning, I didn't bother to look. Instead I swung open the door and caught sight of a tall, thin man I didn't recognize. He was dressed in mud-splattered coveralls with hair that looked like he had just awoken from a weeklong nap. His

Neighborhood Nostalgia 137

gaze was slightly vacuous. There was a splattering noise at his feet. If Jesus had asked me at that moment who my neighbor was, I would have pleaded, "Anyone but this man."

I stood frozen for a few seconds as I looked from the red-black puddle at his feet to the large cut of raw meat dripping blood through his fingers. He reached out his hands, and now the blood was dripping on the welcome mat that greeted visitors to the parsonage. "This is for you," he said, looking down and avoiding my widening eyes.

That was the first time I met Junior. My husband was pastoring a small rural church at the time, and we were enjoying the slow pace of the country in contrast to the bustle of the city we had just left. Usually when there was a knock at the door, it was someone with fresh vegetables from their garden, their "firstfruits" offering to the pastor. But this time it was Junior.

Junior was a bona fide hermit. Except for when he sold the vegetables from his garden to townsfolk or did piecemeal work for local farmers, he rarely had contact with people. A fiftyish bachelor who looked older than he was, Junior lived alone in a dilapidated house that slanted sideways and rested upon dirt floors. It was rumored that electricity and indoor plumbing were modern concoctions he could do without. Junior had worked as a farmhand for one of our deacons and had recently suffered a stroke. At the request of the deacon, my husband had gone to visit and pray with Junior in the hospital, and to show his appreciation, Junior had brought us a gift, venison in its most rudimentary state.

No matter how ill conceived Junior's show of appreciation was he became my neighbor that day. He came to visit a second time, thankfully without a recently departed gift, and was standing in the living room, looking at an old painting I had just bought. I hadn't bothered to replace the cracked glass or refurbish the frame in any way; I liked it worn, still bearing the nicks and scuffs of time. My daughter, Emily, who was four at the time, watched Junior as he looked at the painting. Emily has always had an ethereal quality about her, as if she has a spiritual awareness of things most others aren't privy to and a deep compassion for anyone who is hurting. "My Mommy likes broken things," she said, her eyes moving from the painting to Junior, and then she added, "like you."

Junior *had* been broken by life, and like my distressed frame, no one had bothered to try to repair him. From what we could gather, his parents had either died or left him when he was a boy, and he had been raised by an uncle who had since died, leaving him completely alone. I wonder if my husband was the only visitor who came to see him in the hospital when he suffered a stroke. My husband had found him paging through a Gideon's Bible left in the hospital nightstand. Junior's sudden interest in his own mortality led to further conversation, and together my husband and Junior prayed for new life, eternal life.

A few months after our first meeting, we asked Junior to spend Christmas with us. When I greeted him at the door, the coveralls had been replaced by an old suit jacket, a few sizes too small, his long arms stretching beyond the jacket sleeves, which were ripped in the elbows. He had carefully smoothed down his hair. His wanting to dress up for our celebration deeply touched me; he was the most resplendent Christmas guest we'd ever had. He didn't eat much and left early after complaining of not feeling well, but his presence was the best part of the day for me. "Last night when I lay in bed," I wrote in my journal the next day, "I sensed the Lord giving us a gentle thank you for ministering and feeding Him on Christmas day. That was Jesus Himself in Junior's chair.

Amy Hollingsworth

•••

Sophisticated listening devices are nothing new. They're called "neighbors."

Sam Ewing

•••

MY NEIGHBOR

When I was hungry, you gave me to eat.
When I was thirsty, you gave me to drink.
When I was weary, you helped me find rest.
When I was anxious, you calmed all my fears.
When I was little, you taught me to read.
When I was lonely, you gave me your love.
When I was on a sick bed, you cared for my needs.
In a strange country, you made me at home.
Hurt in a battle, you bound up my wounds.
Searching for kindness, you held out your hand.

Mother Teresa

•••

My neighbors are keeping me broke. They are always buying things I can't afford.

G. K. Chesterton

•••

REMEMBER THE FRANDSENS

The summer that I was twelve, I vacationed at my uncle's ranch in Santa Clara Valley, California. I was a reluctant visitor. That is, until I met Smithy.

Smithy, who lived on the next ranch, was the most forthright and the most completely adult boy I'd ever known. My aunt said it was because Smithy's parents died before he was eight, and a bachelor uncle had had to rear the boy as best he could. My uncle said that hard-working farm boys were usually old for their years, even at twelve.

Becoming friends with Smithy wasn't easy. I soon learned

that the slightest lapse into things either fanciful or childish sent Smithy scurrying. He had an annoying habit of disappearing whenever he got bored or discomfited. My aunt said his real name was Lloyd, but he never admitted it; one called him Smithy, or went unanswered.

When the old Horlick farm was sold, by mail, to an eastern couple named Frandsen, I thought it exciting because I had heard that the new owners were stage people. Smithy remained noncommittal, but on the day I chose to happen to walk up the Frandsen's driveway, Smithy was with me. And when, halfway up the walk, we bumped right into Mr. and Mrs. Frandsen, and they greeted us with exclamations of joy and welcome, Smithy was too surprised to run away.

The newcomers were, I judged, nearly fifty. Mrs. Frandsen had a beautiful, soft face, and her lovely blond hair was just touched with gray. Mr. Frandsen was shorter than his wife, although he held himself exceedingly straight, and his little brown eyes twinkled with kindness.

We were their very first visitors, they said; we must come out of the hot sun and into the cool of the house. Neither Smithy nor I had ever met grownups like this before. We were not used to sitting in front rooms decorated with spears and masks and signed photographs of costumed ladies and gentlemen, nor to being served tea out of something called a samovar.

Most of all, we were not used to being treated as contemporaries. The Frandsens told us exciting anecdotes about New York, about their experiences when they had acted in road companies. We were allowed to glimpse their future plans, the dreams-that-were-going-to-come-true, now that they had retired and settled down.

George—of course we were to call them George and Lisa, were we not their first new friends?—was going to become a real farmer. He had all the government bulletins. Most wonderful of all, the Frandsens were going to adopt a baby. "A baby girl," Lisa said, "with blue eyes."

George beamed. "For months, now, we have had our request in. When we came through San Francisco we filled out final forms."

"And always," Lisa said, "we'll tell her that we chose her." They showed us the books they had about raising babies. Now, as soon as the agency people sent a lady down to inspect them, the baby would be theirs.

Smithy and I stayed on and on. Never had I felt so welcome, such a distinguished guest. I chattered, and no one said it was time for me to go home, or that my mother wanted me. When Lisa tried to get Smithy to talk, too, and asked his name, I—drunk with social success—blurted out that it was Lloyd Smith. Lisa said Lloyd was a fine name. I expected something to happen, but Smithy just rolled his eyes alarmingly, and looked, for a moment, like my uncle's colt.

When we finally stood up to go, George and Lisa said we were to come back often, often, and Lisa kissed my cheek.

I couldn't stay away from the Frandsens. They enchanted me. They called their stove Ophelia, because it was quite, quite mad. They named their bantam rooster Iago; their pig was Falstaff. When we sat on the cool side porch, George and Lisa told me whole plots out of plays, even acted them out. Sometimes I would catch a glimpse of Smithy, out in the orchard, and he would be listening too.

When my uncle's farm dog, Old Ben, died of age, and no one but me was sad about it, I lugged the poor hound's body over to the Frandsens'. Halfway there, Smithy materialized, and took over my burden. He helped George dig a grave of honor at the foot of the Frandsens' pepper tree. After it was all over, Smithy listened quietly while George said the most beautiful words I had ever heard: "Fear no more the heat of the sun, or the furious winter's rages . . ."

As the days went on I despaired of making Lisa understand that Smithy was not a child. When she baked bread she sent him miniature loaves; when she made cake there was always a tiny one, baked in the lid of the baking powder tin, for Smithy. Obediently, I delivered them; silently he pocketed them.

On the Saturday that the agency lady came to inspect the Frandsens I went into the orchard, to be out of the way. I found Smithy there. We each picked a tree, leaned against it, and settled down to wait. I wasn't worried; anyone could see that the Frandsens were remarkable people.

"And the way they do everything," I said, "with—well, with ceremony. Smithy, aren't they wonderful?"

Smithy just grunted. I noticed, though, when we heard the agency lady's car clatter away that he was on his feet as quickly as I. The moment we entered the house, we knew that something was terribly wrong.

Lisa was sitting quietly in a chair. She didn't look gay or young anymore. George patted her shoulder, while he told us.

"We are too old. People past forty-five are not permitted to adopt small babies."

I was indignant. "But they must have known—the forms—"

George looked down. "In the theater, one takes off a year here, a year there. Truly, Lisa and I had forgotten—" he shrugged. "Today we told our true ages. The agency lady is kind, but it is a new rule."

"I can understand," Lisa said bravely. "It is for the child's good. So that—so that a child shall not have old—parents." She began to cry.

I was suddenly aware of being a child, too, without experience or knowledge. I did not know what to say to my friends, how to comfort them. And Smithy was no help. He slipped away without a word.

When, a little later, we heard a thump on the porch, I had the wild hope that it might be the Agency lady coming back. But it was only Smithy. He had his Sunday suit on, and the knickers were too short, and he looked funny. He gave me a terrible frown, and set down three newspaper-wrapped packages and two fishing poles. Standing there in the open doorway, he said matter-of-factly, "People are always adopting children; why can't it be the other way around once in a while?" His voice began to climb. "So I choose you. I asked my uncle, and he doesn't care, because he wants to move to the city anyway. So if you—if you want—"

Lisa ran across the room and put her wet cheek against Smithy's face, and said, "Lloyd! Oh, Lloyd!" I was afraid she was going to try to kiss him, and I wished somebody would shut the door. I guess George understood, because he started shaking Smithy's hand manfully, and saying, "Well, now, welcome, welcome."

Smithy seemed to make some tremendous effort. "Isn't there some sort of ceremony?" he asked George. "Shouldn't you—carry me into the house, or something?"

"But that's a ceremony for—" I started to say, but couldn't finish.

I do not think that twelve-year-old girls are particularly aware of poignancy, but I do know that the scene, that day, touched me beyond tears. Vainly trying to swallow the hurting in my throat, I watched George Frandsen stoop and lift the tall, gangly boy, the long blackstockinged legs awkwardly disposed. Gently, carefully, he carried Smithy over the threshold and into the house.

"Well, now," I heard George say, "well, now, son . . ."

Kathryn Forbes

THE CORNER GROCERY

The corner grocery was a family affair with no budget for advertising, no neon signs and, often, no corner. A simple wooden board with the family name made do. Willis's and Olson's were noted for their meat; Curtis's for fresh vegetables; Campbell's for low-priced canned good; and Harold's—across from the elementary school—for the best penny candies.

Inside, the warmth of wooden floors, shelves, counters, and vegetable crates welcomed young and old. And so did the storekeepers, greeting each customer by name.

Only two or three brands stocked the shelves. Fresh fruits and vegetables were mostly bought in season, with strawberries for shortcake in May, the first watermelon for the Fourth of July, and corn-on-the-cob for weeks after. A white-aproned butcher stood ready to cut beef to order, grind hamburger, or wrap a chosen chicken.

Contrary to modern marketing strategy, items were grouped conveniently. Meat, produce, and milk occupied one area. Baked, canned, boxed, and household products had their own special sections. This arrangement was permanent, and most any kid could find what was needed if he could remember what he came for or if he could read the shopping list. Of course, if he couldn't read it, the grocer's wife, Bessie, would do it for him.

Mothers would complain if sugar went up a penny-a-pound, but their loyalty to the neighborhood corner grocery remained strong. For when times were tight, cash wasn't needed. Family credit "slips" were kept in the cash drawer to be paid on paydays. With a note from Mother, even a child was allowed to sign the back of a slip. This way, children became aware of family finances.

If this accounting method seems unsophisticated, the transaction involving the return of soda pop bottles was not. The bottles, at two cents for regular and five cents for the big ones, were collected by kids and exchanged for penny candy. Jawbreakers, licorice sticks, Double Bubble gum, Hershey's bars, Baby Ruths, Butterfingers, and Three Musketeers ranged from two for a penny to a nickel apiece. Two Pepsi, one Squirt, and one big Coke bottle presented a multitude of possibilities to the indecisive kids and required infinite patience on the part of Bessie.

Patricia Heydenberk

> Summer must be over. My neighbor just returned my lawn furniture.
>
> G. K. Chesterton

THE AUCTIONEER

It had been 40 years since I'd driven those back roads and memories flooded as the once-proud house I remembered from childhood came into view.

Suffocating blackberry vines now clambered up its gingerbread-topped porch pillars; holes sprinkled its back-broken roof; clapboard siding gaped to accommodate nest-seeking raccoons. Yet, amazingly, it still stood.

Suddenly a vignette from twenty years before surfaced on my mental screen: Ella, stiff and weather-beaten even then, stood by the screen door with its flapping dish towel drying on the spring. Her dim eyes squinted, surveying the scene which had brought city people searching for the advertised "Sale of Choice Antiques."

The portly, cowboy-hatted auctioneer mounted a podium and began his spiel: "What am I offered for this old-fashioned afghan? Thirty, thirt. . . . thirt . . . thirty-five . . . . going, going. . . ."

Then, warming up and quickening his pace: "Next a jen-you-wine, an-teek washboard, gair-inteed to get your clothes clean!" His drone went on: "Forty, fort, fort . . . do I hear fifty?

"SOLD! Come get it, lady."

I remembered Ella from my childhood years. Her Jeb was born in that same house 83 years before. He'd brought his bride there, fathered nine children, tilled the surrounding land.

But Jeb had died and their lifetime of belongings was being auctioned off. It was a carnival scene: tables with balloons and signs, SANDWICHES FOR SALE, children running and yelling, coffee odors mingling with that of cigarettes. Jeb never smoked; he'd not be a "stumbling block" to anyone.

Buyers' interest heightened with, "Who'll start the bid on this 100-year-old grandfather clock?"

Another stirring of excitement at, "Next this antique, brass-bound trunk. . . ." It had held Ella's wedding gown, a dead infant's button-topped shoes, her cherished lusterware pitcher.

Suddenly the scene became too personal, too intimate to watch, and, back then, I had to turn away from the auctioneer and the bargain hunters who'd clustered, like crows, to pick at remnants of a couple's lifetime belongings.

Now, forty years later, as I again viewed the house—dilapidated and beaten by the elements—I remembered the elderly couple. "Senior citizens" we call them now—there are no "old people" anymore. "Good folk" the neighbors said of them.

Half a century they'd labored, raised children, paid their bills, gone to church, read their Bibles, prayed. Even when they lost a son, hail wiped out one year's crop and brought drought the next, they'd never doubted God.

As I was reminiscing, it seemed I again heard another auctioneer's voice—this one belonging to the Master Auctioneer: "Now, here's a rarity these days . . . an old-fashioned marriage that's lasted for fifty years. What will you bid for it?

"And another antique on my sales block: Faith. You don't see much of it these days, either. This antique will take you through thick and thin. You, over there. . . . What will you offer?

"Look at this out-of-date oldie: Believing my promise, 'I will never leave thee nor forsake thee.' Any bids on it?

"What are such treasures worth to you? Do I hear bids? No . . . sorry, Sir. Sorry, Ma'am. . . . I don't accept cash, check or credit cards. 'Why?' you ask. Well, they can't be bought, you see; they're gifts; they come only by complete trust in Me."

Isabel Torrey

Neighborhood Nostalgia 147

Wife: I'm happy to see that the neighbors finally returned our lawn mower before they moved. They certainly had it long enough.

Husband: Our lawn mower? I just bought it at the garage sale they're having.

Bob Phillips

"Yes, sir, there is a way to stop telemarketers from calling you during dinner. Don't eat dinner."

A young business woman was approached by a real estate agent who wanted to sell her a home. "A home? I was born in a hospital, educated in a boarding school, courted in a car, married in church. We eat in restaurants, spend our mornings playing golf, and spend our afternoons playing bridge at the club. Evenings we go to the movies, and when I die I'm going to be buried from a funeral home. I don't need a home; all I need is a garage!"

Albert Stauderman

••

MY SARI LIFE

When our family left our Virginia home of fifteen years to relocate in another state, I walked around with a lump in my throat and a hollow feeling in my heart. But I knew the quickest remedy to my homesickness was to meet some people and hopefully to make new friends in the process.

So, just days after settling in our new thirty-year-old apartment, I made several loaves of banana bread, put on my walking shoes, and prepared to meet the neighbors. I envisioned myself exchanging polite and witty conversation with blond soccer moms in Gap sweatshirts and white leather Keds. I would ask about their children—children with names like Tristan, Chloe, and Sterling. We would plan to have coffee once a week and perhaps even collect donations together for worthy charities. *I can do this!* I mentally coached myself before heading out the door.

The moment my sneaker set foot in the shared entryway, a pungent odor assailed my nose. Since it turned out to be permanent, our family came to call it "the smell." We surmised that it was some combination of curry, entrails, and fish heads. Regardless, my banana bread would clearly go begging.

Slightly unnerved, I knocked on Door Number One. A turban-wearing gentleman named Mohammed greeted me, flashing a shiny gold tooth with his smile. Behind Door Number Two: a sari-clad woman cradling a baby with a shock of black hair; and behind Door Number Three: a spry, elderly woman who spoke no English. She ushered me to her balcony, where she was roasting a small animal on a spit. I looked below to the tree-filled courtyard and noticed nary a squirrel in sight.

I quickly realized Dorothy wasn't in Kansas anymore and Toto was barking in broken English. When I pulled into the carpool line for the first time at Trevor's grade school, I felt like belting out, "It's a Small World After All." The student body represented thirty nationalities. At "International Culture Night," my banana bread went hoof-to-hoof with curried goat for a blue ribbon.

Although being a fish out of water (or a stranger in my own country) was difficult at first, I grew to appreciate this unique environment—my own neighborhood U.N. And after nearly two years, I'd made friends with Ani from Armenia, Radika from Romania, and Kristy from Korea. Amazingly, none wore Keds or had a precocious child named Sterling. But we found a common bond in sharing mothers' love for our children while looking out for them in a fast-changing, multicultural world. It was a major growth experience for me.

Rachel St. John–Gilbert

SHAVING MUGS

Some of my favorite memories from childhood involve time spent alone with my dad. In a family of six children—five brothers and me—time alone with either parent did not come that often; and when it did, since I was the only girl, it was usually with my mom, who often took me along on Sunday afternoon trips to the movies, or shopping, or for an ice cream sundae. But it was time with Dad that I craved. My spirits would soar when he'd invite me to walk with him to the barbershop on a Saturday morning.

We lived in a residential neighborhood of a large city, and my dad's barbershop was just three blocks away. Right next door was the bakery, where we always stopped on the way—a donut for me and coffee for him. While we walked, Dad would ask about school or tell me stories about when he was a boy in that very same neighborhood. Inside the barbershop, he would sit me on one of the old, black vinyl couches with my donut while he took his own place in the barber's chair for his "regular men's haircut." There were always a couple of men Dad knew from the neighborhood, and they would talk—about politics and about baseball, mostly. Sometimes they would slip into the Greek they had all learned as boys but was incomprehensible to me. That was for my benefit, to hide the things unfit for my ears. I didn't care, I just loved being there. This was my father's world, and I felt proud to be included.

> This was my father's world, and I felt proud to be included.

These warm memories of that old barbershop led me to start collecting shaving mugs. Although my father did his shaving at home with an electric razor, the very first time I laid eyes on an old, personalized shaving mug in a tiny antique shop, I thought of him and of those Saturday mornings together. I asked the woman in the shop about the mug, and she explained that it was what was called an "occupational" shaving mug because it displayed the owner's name and an image symbolic of his trade. This mug had belonged to someone named "C. Alexander," who was, judging by the printing press pictured on its side, employed in the business of printing. The shopkeeper explained to me that in the days when men went to the barbershop daily for a shave, the barber would keep each customer's soap and brush in a personalized mug. When men started shaving at home with disposable safety razors, the practice went out of style and made the daily stop at the barbershop unnecessary. Shaving mugs had become a relic of an era gone by, a popular collectible, a piece of history. I bought the mug, sold less by the shopkeeper's talk of collectibles than by the tug

Neighborhood Nostalgia

of my own memories. But after I had it at home on my shelf, I started to think about how much my father would have enjoyed the days when a daily trip to the barbershop was a necessity. He had loved his old neighborhood and liked the feeling of knowing who lived where and who did what. He would have relished the chance to sit and talk every morning while the barber took care of his shave. Not long after I brought that first mug home, I came across another in the same small antique shop. I bought that one, too. This had belonged to "A. Hawkins," who had been a firefighter. I have recently added a third mug to my collection, that of Francis Clarke, an undertaker.

I have a special shelf in my family room reserved for my small but growing collection of shaving mugs. Many visitors have remarked that it seems an unlikely collection for a woman of my age, someone quite far removed by years and gender from the days of barbershop shaves. That may be, but in truth the collection is not a tribute to shaving practices of old, but to my dad. When I look at that row of mugs, I remember those special Saturday mornings, how proud I felt as I listened to him talk with his friends, and I remember the greatest lesson my father taught me: that I was someone special to him.

Isabella Grayson

••

The Bible tells us to love our neighbors and also to love our enemies, probably because they are generally the same people. *Bob Phillips*

Dr. Ned Wiley loves to tell of preaching during his seminary days in a small rural church on Mother's Day. An old lady, very hard of hearing, was encouraging him along audibly, with such expressions as "That's right."

Near the end, to dramatize mother love, he made a cross of himself and said, "If I were hanged on the highest hill, Mother of mine, Mother of mine . . ." The old lady, not hearing too well, croaked out, "Lord, grant it!"

Helen and Larry Eisenberg

My neighbor is such a hypochondriac that he filled his water bed with chicken soup.

Caskie Stinnet

"WELL, ALL THE NEIGHBORHOOD DOORBELLS WORK!"

The man in the repair shop said, "Here it is, Mr. Wilson. Your lawnmower is now in perfect condition. Just one precaution, however. Don't ever lend it to a neighbor."

"That's just the trouble," said Mr. Wilson. "I am the neighbor."

Bob Phillips

THE WALK TO SCHOOL

I have always felt sorry for children who miss the experience of walking to school.

When I was a small town youngster we walked at least a mile each way, whatever the weather. And the distance was fraught with wonder, no matter how familiar its landmarks became.

On certain corners there were magic talismans to be invoked—simple lettering on the sidewalk immortalizing some builder's name. Yet the first one to stamp on them and shout, "Good luck!" was sure to be protected from evil all day.

And there were houses that loomed with significance en route. There was the Flower Lady whose entire yard was a riot of blossoms and who might give you some for your teacher if she felt in a generous mood. . . .

There was the sheriff's house; he could arrest you and throw you in jail if he chose, the older kids claimed. . . .

There was the Witch's House, an ancient red brick with cupolas and towers, where a daft old lady lived; she sometimes sang from a window, or scurried out in her little white cap to ask if you'd seen her angels who'd flown off again.

There was the Presbyterian Church with its mighty chimes and clock, and its bubbling drinking fountain. . . .

There was that whispering treasure house, the public library. On the way home you could stop and borrow exactly two books, no more. But by starting them as you sauntered along, you could have them read by tomorrow and borrow two more.

In the fall there was the scent of apple orchards and the dusty scuff and rattle of fallen leaves. You picked up the loveliest samples, scarlet maple, golden beech, to show your teacher, then pin on a paper to trace.

When the first snow fell, you raced joyously through it, trying to catch the cool lacy flakes on your tongue. Drifts did not deter you. They were an excuse to wade.

Snow and ice held the earth fast most of winter, followed by a miracle when the warm days came. For now the gutters ran wild with the melted waters, and sidewalks mirrored an upside-down world of sky and clouds and trees. And gazing down, down, you felt a breathless transporting.

You were one of the five foolish princesses who ran off at night into the world beneath the world and danced their slippers to shreds.

You spied the first robin on your way to school. And the first crocus, and it was news. And there were seedpods to be stepped on; how they squirted. And the fuzz of cottonwoods to catch, and dandelion fluff to be blown. And violets to be gathered in a shady wood, and clover to be braided. And you bounced balls, skipped ropes, and raced to join friends who were waiting, or they rushed up to join you. And you argued and philosophized and giggled and dreamed big dreams as you made this daily pilgrimage.

There was time for these things, to think and wonder and truly be a child on these long walks to school.

Marjorie Holmes

MOVING DAY

It took nearly a week to drive all of our possessions and our two children across the country from Chicago to Phoenix for my husband's new job. It had been an exhausting trip, and we were nearly out of both money and energy. But the worst was ahead of us.

The day we moved into our new home happened to fall on Thanksgiving Day. All of our family and friends lived in the Midwest, so the four of us unloaded the truck ourselves. It was no small job. My four-year-old son pulled smaller things in his wagon, and my eight-year-old daughter carried a steady supply of lighter boxes. It bothered me to have to ask them to work with us, especially on a holiday. We had been working since early morning without a break. We were getting slower and slower.

"You doing okay?" my husband would ask regularly as we struggled up the steps with the couch or a mattress.

"I'm fine. You?"

"Yep."

Other than that, conversation was nonexistent. Even though no one said so, I could tell we were all starting to feel sorry for ourselves. We were stuck doing all this backbreaking work on a day that families are supposed to be feasting and playing together. We weren't feeling very grateful as we started our new life.

At 2:30 in the afternoon, we still hadn't stopped for lunch, but no one was complaining about being hungry. I think we all just wanted to get the job finished. I had just started to wonder where we could go to get something to eat on Thanksgiving Day. I was also praying to myself, *Father, I believe You brought us here safely, and You will also take care of us.* I set down the box of books I was carrying, sighed, and headed back to the truck for more.

That's when I saw a man walking up the sidewalk. "Time for a break," he said, smiling. He introduced himself as our neighbor. "You folks need to come on over and get some lunch. We just finished eating and we have so many leftovers. Everything's on the table waiting for you."

My husband and I hesitated, but the kids started cheering.

Seeing we needed a little more convincing, he said, "I just moved here myself a couple months ago, from Georgia. I know exactly what you're going through. While we've been cooking, we've been watching you work. To be honest, you folks are starting to drag a little, and you all need to come get some nourishment. These kids need to eat!"

He was right. We followed him to his home and were met by his daughters, two babies, and a few other relatives. We lost our shyness the minute we smelled the food. Sliced turkey with all the trimmings was laid out on the table.

The amazing thing is, it didn't end there. We had been back to work for a couple of hours when he showed up again. "Okay, folks, we're having dessert now. You need to come over for some pie," our neighbor said. We felt we had imposed enough, but he insisted.

One good meal with a huge helping of kindness can really change your perspective! We suddenly felt as if our Father had gathered us, His well-loved children, into His arms for comfort. We thanked our Comforter for whispering in our neighbor's ear the words that caused him to open his heart and his home to us.

A few weeks later I tried to express in a card what our neighbor's kindness meant to us. The cookies I baked just didn't seem like thanks enough. Then it dawned on me that feeling as if my thanks were inadequate was perhaps the beginnings of true gratitude, the kind that humbles you. It stirs in you a desire to give to others from your place of blessing, to attempt to make someone else feel what you have felt.

My neighbor's act of generosity, a beautiful reminder of God's faithfulness, changed the way I look at those around me. As I start my new life here, I want to keep that giving spirit alive by being more aware of people who might also be in need of some nourishment—for body *and* soul.

Brenda Sprague

Neighborhood Nostalgia

First neighbor: We are going to move. We're going to be living in a better neighborhood.
   Second neighbor: So are we.
   First neighbor: Oh, are you also moving?
   Second neighbor: No, we're staying right here.
Bob Phillips

We make our friends; we make our enemies, but God makes our next-door neighbour.
G. K. Chesterton

"There's really not much to tell. I just grew up and married the girl next door."

> The best thing about an air conditioner is that the neighbors can't borrow it.
>
> **Great Thoughts**

ALL ABOUT BUBBLE GUM

The way you tell a real great kid,
The way you tell a chum,
Is after he's chewed it for a while,
You get his bubble gum.

Alas, history failed to record the name of the poet who wrote these noble lines. But he was obviously an expert observer of two phenomena: kids and bubble gum—with maybe some penny candy thrown in. The only real bubble-gum experts are kids: the two have gone together since 1906, when "the gum that blew up" first appeared on the American scene.

In the days of my own childhood we were loyal to only one bubble gum: Fleers—tough, chewy pink stuff that came wrapped as "kisses" with twisted paper tails. When you untwisted them, out popped the Fleers Dubble Bubble Kids.

Only in the direst emergencies would we opt for Brand X, usually a gumball dispensed by machine. It was small and cost a penny when a penny was a fortune. And it wasn't as durable as the delicious pink stuff. It did blow bubbles, of course, and still does, even though last year's sugar shortage nearly ended penny candy and gum in America. We might have had a pint-sized revolution if kids had only known about an even grimmer crisis. It had to do with the oil shortage; since petroleum is one base for gum. Its shortage almost finished the job that a lack of sugar had started . . . but now let's go back to the fun!

Remember the furious bubble-blowing contests held in

schoolyards in the '40s? I do. There was "Puff" McAdder (name changed because he's now a politician and I don't want to give him a free plug!) who blew a bubble as big as a beach ball. Even I, the school pygmy, achieved bubbles of basketball proportions, only to be vanquished by blowhards who almost certainly practiced in their sleep.

Teachers responsible for our well-being—read "neatness"—threw their hands up in horror after those gummy games when we entered classrooms latex-laden, mostly on our faces. And what could be more wonderful than chasing a pack of screaming girls while holding a pink and well-chewed wad ready to stick in their hair?

Pennies weren't from heaven in those days either, so cadging grew to a fine art. Most of us knew dozens of ways, not all of them sanitary, to scavenge a free chew. First, and least desirable, was the direct approach, which soon taught us a thing or two about friendship. A so-so friend would hem and haw and maybe give you a chaw. An enemy would laugh—and maybe punch you—in your face. A really good friend would take his wad out of his mouth while it still had some sugar in it and allow you a few blissful chews before reclaiming it!

And did we come up with some unbelievable storage places! Under the table (done surreptitiously at suppertime when parents weren't looking). Snugged against door moldings. Stuck to bed rails. Wedged behind our ears—the list is endless.

If you want someone to blame for this terrible vice, blame the ancient Greeks. They weren't forever blowing bubbles, but they chewed gum—or at least a substance called *mastiche* (Greek for "to chew") that came from the resin of a tree. A physician named Dioscorides even claimed it had curative powers.

By AD 200 the Mayans were at it too, chomping the coagulated juice of the sapodilla tree; the stuff later became known as chicle. The Mayans disappeared, but their descendants kept chicle-chewing alive well into the 19th century.

American Indians had spruce gum. And as a kid on a Texas farm I chewed "sweet gum," only it wasn't sweet; it was like biting an inner tube soaked in turpentine. We also mauled chunks of paraffin left over from sealing jelly jars. Later, in the city, we discovered the delights of road tar, foul, dirty, and darkly satisfying. We could even black out our incisors with it and pretend the bully on the block had removed our front teeth, which brought anguished shrieks from our mothers and I'm-glad-smarty grins from our sisters.

Modern gum was born in the United States about 1869, thanks to General Santa Anna. He had contacted American inventor Thomas Adams hoping the man could turn chicle into a substitute for rubber. The general arrived chewing the stuff, and Adams immediately saw it was superior to any then-known chewing-gum base. In a few years, Adams' Chiclets began appearing on the scene.

Chicle is basically latex. Some latexes—*latex* being a generic term—are *sorva* and *leche caspi* from the Amazon Valley; *tunu* and *nispero* from Central America, and *jelutong*, found in Malaya and Indonesia. But juice from the 100-foot-tall sapodilla tree of the Yucatan Peninsula is still the main source of chicle. Tapped only after they're a quarter-century old, a cutting yields about two-and-a-half pounds of gum base, and it's three years before they can be "bled" again.

And, oh yes, you could also get real Baby Ruths and Snickers and Three Musketeers bars for a penny.

I never could get enough candy. I swore to best friends, who joined me in my oath, that when I grew up I'd have all the candy that I ever wanted. But life is full of surprises. How could I know then that I'd change, as we all do?

As little boys, we love candy. As grown men in a world that sometimes seems unhappy, sometimes insecure and unfamiliar, surely it isn't odd that we wonder if we can still have even a little of that Willy Wonka world.

And if we find it, is it worth more than a penny?

William Childress

THE PEOPLE WHO USED TO LIVE HERE

*H*ave you ever felt that sometimes when you buy a house you buy a family with it?

It may be the family that has just packed up and is departing as you (feeling a bit shy and strange, almost the apologetic intruder) move your own crew in. For a little while the ghosts of this former family linger. You find them popping out at you from closets and cupboards—in a sash from a little red dress that still dangles on a hook, a garden hat, a book, a sheaf of accounts, a forgotten toy.

The personality of your predecessor seems to be watching as you get acquainted with her sink, her stove, hang curtains at what were once her windows. "No, no, not that way, stupid," you nervously fancy her scolding. And unconsciously defend, "Look, it's my house now, and you'll be surprised at the improvements I'll make."

Then you laugh at your own absurdity—feeling rivals, imagine!—and something warm and nice comes over you as you see that she's left a casserole in the refrigerator, a list of baby sitters, and those bedroom draperies you admired.

In most cases they leave rather quickly, these forerunners who lived here. They fade, they vanish, you forget that this roof and these walls ever sheltered anyone else. No matter how often the neighbors refer to them, or how many preceded you, there is the conviction that this house now firmly and forever has been yours.

Yet in an old house, this is not always the case. A very old house that another family built long ago when the neighborhood was new, and lived in fully and richly until they went their separate ways and the house fell into impersonal hands. And though we have lived here twelve years now, I sometimes wonder if the huge old house we occupy will ever fully and completely belong to us. For they were waiting for us in the attic the day we came, those gracious ladies and gentlemen of the past.

They smiled at us from their photographs. And when we plunged into ancient trunks that had obviously been many times around the world, we found even more graphic evidence—for there, enchantingly, were their bustles and bonnets and high-button shoes and tall silk hats.

Many of their letters they left behind them too. Invitations and bits of small talk written in fine and elegant script. Magic lantern slides taken in Egypt, the Philippines, Japan. Diplomas. Citations.

And though they have all been gone for many years now, neighbors—old neighbors who knew them at the height of their prominence, still speak of them. And their words are filled with admiration and affection. "Oh, yes, everybody knew the Corbetts." And people still refer to the house where we live as "The Corbett House."

And one day, to our joy and amazement, some of them, living people, not ghosts at all, but vivid young descendants, came swarming in. And expressed astonishment and delight that we had actually saved some of those souvenirs of their ancestral past.

"Well, we just couldn't bear to throw them out," we admitted. "After building the house and living in it so many years—well, it sort of seemed as if your family, as well as its house, belonged to us."

Marjorie Holmes

We can live without our friends but not without our neighbors.
Thomas Fuller

8

Outside the City Limits

Just outside the city limits of most any town or city are happenings and people who like being a little outside the limits of standard behavior. These provide the rest of us ample opportunities for a good laugh.

My son Lincoln and I had been to the town of Frankenmuth, Michigan, to fish. He was about eleven at the time. The town is only about fifty miles from Flint, where we lived, and is nearly world famous for its breweries and for Zenders—a national monument to fried chicken and sauerbraten. It is much less well known for salmon fishing, but that's why we went there. The Clinton River is dammed there, and the Lake Huron salmon collect below the dam.

We drove over right after school, hoping to fish a couple of hours before dark. It was late fall. When we headed home after a very successful trip, it was cold and very dark. We were speeding along a narrow, twisting country road, when suddenly my headlights revealed a white duck in the middle of the road. I can't imagine what it was doing in the road at that time of night. I thought ducks were like chickens and went to sleep as soon as it got dark—and this one should have. I was going much too fast to swerve, and there was no time to stop. I heard the sickening whack and crunch of the duck hitting the underside of the car repeatedly.

It isn't easy to explain my next action—in fact, it's a little embarrassing—but I have to try, or I can't tell the rest of the story. You need to know me personally, and you need to understand the way I was brought up. In my family, nothing was ever wasted. It was a sin to waste.

I turned around and went back to pick up the duck so we could take it home and eat it. It was lying in a heap, sprawled out in obvious death in the middle of ten thousand feathers. I pulled up alongside, reached out my door, picked up the duck, laid it on the floor behind my seat, and headed home once again.

Lincoln was very quiet as we drove, but completely alert. Normally, he would have been sound asleep after such a day, but the incident with the duck had totally captured his imagination. I noticed that he kept looking behind my seat. A few minutes later, he said, "Dad, do ducks have souls?"

"No, Son, ducks don't have souls."

"What happens to a duck when it dies?"

"We eat it."

"I mean, where does it go?"

"It doesn't go anywhere. It just *isn't* anymore."

"Oh." He thought for a few minutes and then he said, "Dad, is it OK to pray for a duck?"

"I guess so, but why would you want to?"

"I feel sorry for it."

He lapsed into a thoughtful silence, and I assumed that he was praying. He kept his eyes on the duck, and a few minutes later, he spoke again.

"Dad?"

"What, Son?"

"God just answered my prayer; that duck's alive."

"Son, that duck is dead."

A few minutes passed.

"Dad, the duck is alive. I just saw it move."

"No, Son, the duck may have moved from the motion of the car, but that duck is not alive. I know you feel sorry for the duck, and I do too. And I know you prayed for the duck, but we have to learn to accept bad things in life. *The duck is dead.* You heard it hit the car, didn't you?"

"Yes, but Dad, the duck just moved again, and it's not the motion of the car. *It's looking right at me.*"

"Son, this has gone far enough. You mustn't allow your imagination to run away with you. I've told you that the duck is dead. *It is dead!* No amount of wishful thinking can bring it back. Trust me. I'm your father, and when I tell you that the duck is dead, you can believe me.

The duck is dead!

Now, I don't want to hear any more about that duck."

"Yes, sir."

"Quack."

"What was that noise?"

"I think it was the dead duck, Dad."

I turned around, and sure enough, there was the duck, standing up and looking rather puzzled by its new surroundings.

"Son," I said, "it must be a miracle, because that duck was dead!"

We took it home, fed it, found a marvelous place for it to stay—in our swimming pool, which was closed for the winter anyway—and we named her (I guess it was a her) Gertrude. About a month later we went back to Frankenmuth. We took Gertrude and released her as near to the spot where we had found her as possible and went on our way.

I learned a lesson from Gertrude the duck that day. I learned that I'm not always right. I learned that older isn't always wiser, I learned that sometimes we allow our presuppositions to override obvious facts, and I learned that if I insist on being right and won't even listen to another point of view, I might be forced to acknowledge my fallibility by a loud "quack" of reality.

The next time you feel compelled to stand your ground, no matter the fact, just remember Gertrude the duck and relax a little. Learn the grace of laughing at yourself. It really isn't so bad to admit that you're wrong—once in a while.

John William Smith

LISTEN TO THE FIDDLER

Some time ago, while driving through the South, a detour took us from our fast, planned route. Annoyed at the time we were losing, my husband and I barely noticed the beauty of the rural countryside we were driving through.

It was a long detour. The country road climbed soft hills and wound through tiny towns where children and adults often stared openly at the stream of cars bearing out-of-state license plates.

The sun was quickly dipping behind the trees when my husband conceded that we'd have to stop for gas at the next station. "But I guess we'll just have to wait for dinner until we hit the highway again," he said.

About a mile down the road, an ancient, solitary gas pump suddenly appeared in a small clearing that housed two weathered buildings. On one a sign said GAS; the other simply stated FOOD.

The proprietor kept up a friendly conversation, filling our gas tank while we got out to stretch. The aroma wafting from the lunchroom was more than I could bear. "How's the food?" I asked hesitantly. The answer came back full of pride and confidence. 'Mary's the best cook in these parts."

"I can vouch for that," came still another voice, and I turned to see an old gentleman sitting back on a tilted chair in the shadow of a lean-to. He held a penknife and a piece of wood in his hand. "Mary's got country ham today. You wouldn't want to miss that, would you?"

I hesitated, looking at my husband. "We're in a hurry and have already lost time through this detour."

The old man chuckled and shifted in his seat. "You traveling folks are always in a hurry," he said. "I can't see what's more important on a fine evening like this than to set down to a slab of country ham. Unless it'd be to listen to the fiddler."

"The fiddler?" I asked.

"Dance tonight," he said, and pointed a half-finished whistle toward the road we'd just left. "Best fiddler in the country is comin'. You ought to stop awhile and listen to the fiddler."

I looked at the peaceful countryside. The gas-station man was obviously in no hurry; his wife inside was dishing up buttermilk biscuits and baked ham. An old man was enjoying the evening air while only a few yards away the unheeding travelers were rushing past.

So we stayed that evening and stuffed ourselves on Mary's country food. Later we all walked comfortably down the country road to the barn dance. There, people merrily danced to the fiddler's gay music, and later, even my husband and I joined them on the dance floor.

How long had it been since I ambled down a road, stopped to watch the moon on its climb to the top of pines and listened to cicadas and crickets in the night? How many other things was I missing in my hurried life?

Our scheduled vacation was shortened that year by seven hours because of the detour. Seven hours that changed my life. Now when I find myself hurrying too much and repeating, "I just don't have time," I've only to stop and think back to the little clearing and an old man to bring my life back into perspective.

"You really ought to stop," he's saying, "and listen to the fiddler."

Norene Jones

ROADSIDE MEMORIES

Those who see the countryside only as they rush by on the highway miss the chance to enjoy nature at its serene best and to make more discoveries in an hour than they might in a year. In my lifetime, some of the moments I treasure most were spent strolling leisurely along an unpaved country road, with its bordering fences and unspoiled abundance of flora and fauna.

Still vivid in my memory are the visits to my uncle's farm. When I was old enough to leave the yard, I would wander down the dead-end, narrow dirt road across from the house. I have only to shut my eyes, and I'm back there. It is a clear day in July, and it would be hot except for the breeze from Lake Michigan, a few miles away.

The road is magical to a city boy, though it is no more than a pair of dusty ruts with a ridge of grass, dandelions, and plantain between. How many trips have wagon wheels and Model T tires made down this lane, I wonder, to cause such deep tracks?

As I walk, a chipmunk, tail erect, scurries across my path and into a thick tangle of grapevines covering the ground. Experimentally, I tug at some leaves where the animal disappeared, and the whole mass of grapevines moves. Some vines are also clinging by tendrils to the weathered silver-gray wooden posts and rusty barbed wire of the fence, and I can see the clusters of grapes that are forming. Butter-and-eggs, like miniature yellow and orange snapdragons, line the road on either side, much more hardy and profuse than their larger cousins in our garden at home. Rising from the undergrowth are huge bunches of cornflowers and daisies. Spotted white cabbage butterflies flit from one blossom to the next. The breeze pauses momentarily, and I am suddenly aware of the buzzing of honeybees and the deeper droning of bumblebees all along the roadside. Shimmering dragonflies skim erratically over velvety cattails where the road goes past a little marshy area. Across the way, a few monarch butterflies hover around a patch of milkweed. The noisy twittering of a flock of sparrows in a hawthorn tree just over the fence draws my attention, and nearby I see graceful Queen Anne's lace and stalks of blue chicory.

Though I have enjoyed the pleasures of similar roadside worlds many times throughout the years, that special afternoon a half-century ago is always there in memory—vivid and peaceful and warm.

Donald Henning

HOMETOWN

The town I knew when I was small
Had nestled close beside the shore.
It wasn't very big at all—
A single street of store and shops,
Some churches, schools, and growing crops,
Smoke curling from home chimney tops;
Such was the town I knew.

The town I knew was never rushed,
Sunrise was beautiful and bright,
Sunset was glorious and hushed.
The people were a friendly sort
Not given to unkind retort

Main Street Mirth

Nor swayed by slanderous report;
Such was the town I knew.

The town I knew had two long piers
Where steamboats came across the bay,
And I can see yet through the years
A short train pull around the bend,
Stop here and there, and slowly wend
Its way to that pier journey's end;
Such was the town I knew.

The town I knew was quiet, too,
After the steamboat steamed away;
So still that I hear yet today
The rattle of a loosened plank,
A seaman's call, a chain's rude clank,
A boat's swish as it rose and sank;
Such was the town I knew.

The town I knew, today is gone;
In fifty years the tide has turned.
Self-service travel has returned,
Small pleasure craft now line the shore,
Steamboats and railroad are no more,
But in my dreams, just as before
The town I knew lives on.

C. A. Lufburrow

••

A psychiatrist was examining a country patient, a farmer who seemed not overburdened with "the smarts." He began to ask questions. "What's the opposite of sorrow?"

"Easy, Doc . . . joy."
"And the opposite of misery?"
"Even easier, Doc . . . happiness."

The physician was surprised and pleased. "You're doing great. Now tell me the opposite of woe."

"Giddyap!"

James W. Myers

"Quick! Get your gun, Pa! Here come the suburbs."

> I consider it the best part of an education to have been born and brought up in the country.
> *Louisa May Alcott*

A preacher went home with a farm family for dinner. The good wife served the customary preacher dinner: chicken, two young roosters. The preacher lived up to his reputation and ate a large portion.

After the meal the father and the preacher went to the back yard to stretch a little. An old rooster jumped up on the fence and began to crow. Whereupon, the preacher remarked: "You know, that rooster is crowing like he has something to be proud of."

The old man replied, "He does. Two of his sons just entered the ministry."

Leroy Brownlow

ROADSIDE RHYME

Remember the roads of the not-too-distant past and those leisurely rides through the country in your roomy DeSoto? Ah, those country roads—those narrow two-laners that jostled us with potholes and slowed us down with hairpin curves and an endless procession of small towns. As we came around a bend, a small town in sight, speed limits dropped from 45 to 35 to 25, even 15 mph if schoolchildren were around. Then, before we could say, "25, 35, 45," we were breezing across the countryside again, sooner or later to be held up behind a tractor pulling a haywagon through a no-passing zone.

All the same, the pace of the country road was pleasant. Remember how the telephone poles whispered to us as we rolled along absorbing all that we could through a car window? And one thing we didn't mind slowing down for was a little roadside rhyme, courtesy of Burma-Shave. For more than three decades, Burma-Shave signs were a welcome source of roadside amusement, as well as a stroke of advertising genius. For those who don't remember them, they were a series of small road signs that unfolded a clever rhyme or a jaunty jingle to advertise shaving cream.

The man behind the signs was Allan Odell of Minneapolis, Minnesota. Exasperated as a traveling salesman, Odell glimpsed his pot of gold at the end of the rainbow on a road between Aurora and Joliet, Illinois. He happened to drive by a set of small signs advertising a nearby gas station and leading him directly to the station's front door. Why not sell shaving cream that way, thought Odell. So, in 1926, with a set of experimental signs lining a highway outside of Minneapolis, he put Burma-Shave on the road to becoming a national brand.

At first the signs were simply advertisements: SHAVE THE MODERN WAY / FINE FOR THE SKIN / DRUGGISTS HAVE IT / BURMA-SHAVE. As the signs became more numerous, they also became more humorous: FOR PAINTING / COWSHED / BARN OR FENCE / THAT SHAVING BRUSH / IS JUST IMMENSE. The rise of competitive brands of shaving cream and the introduction of the electric razor inspired this suggestion: GIVE THE GUY / THE TOE OF YOUR BOOT / WHO TRIES / TO HAND YOU / A SUBSTITUTE FOR / BURMA-SHAVE. Romantic rhymes played with the allure of a clean-shaven face: HE HAD THE RING / HE HAD THE FLAT / BUT SHE FELT HIS CHIN / AND THAT / WAS THAT.

Public safety messages appeared in 1935: DON'T TAKE A CURVE / AT 60 PER / WE HATE TO LOSE / A CUSTOMER. Clever spoofs prompted many a driver to be more attentive: AT INTER-

SECTIONS / LOOK EACH WAY / A HARP SOUNDS NICE / BUT IT'S HARD TO PLAY. Some of the public service jingles extended beyond the highway. Smokey Bear must have been pleased with: MANY A FOREST / USED TO STAND / WHERE A / LIGHTED MATCH / GOT OUT OF HAND.

Each rhyme was presented, a line at a time, on four or five signs positioned about 30 yards apart, and each was followed by a final sign bearing the Burma-Shave logo. Such a presentation proved to be very effective advertising; it held the attention of its audience as motorists invariably slowed down to read the verses. Furthermore, the appealing little rhymes replayed themselves in the minds of their readers, much like a favorite song. They provided relief, amusement, and, often, a moment of expectant joy as a youngster awaited his turn to read the next group of signs to fellow passengers.

An endless supply of new jingles was ensured by a yearly contest awarding $100 to each writer whose lines were selected for roadside use. Between 1926 and 1963, over 7,000 sets of Burma-Shave signs graced the nation. While the size and color of the signs changed from time to time, the humor remained the same:

1930: HALF A POUND / FOR HALF A DOLLAR / AT THE DRUG STORE / SIMPLY HOLLER / BURMA-SHAVE
1940: HE'S THE BOY / THE GALS FORGOT / HIS LINE / WAS SMOOTH / HIS CHIN WAS NOT
1950: VIOLETS ARE BLUE / ROSES ARE PINK / ON GRAVE / OF THOSE / WHO DRIVE AND DRINK
1960: BEN / MET ANN / MADE A HIT / NEGLECTED BEARD / BEN-ANNA SPLIT

Although Burma-Shave signs have yielded now to flashier billboards and neon displays, their roadside rhymes live on in the memories of many. As for advertising, no gimmick lasts forever; few have lasted as long. Fortunately, road signs are not the only way to sell shaving cream: OUR FORTUNE / IS YOUR/ SHAVEN FACE / IT'S OUR BEST / ADVERTISING SPACE / BURMA-SHAVE.

Kathy Halgren

The farmer had been taken so many times by the local car dealer that when the dealer wanted to buy a cow, the farmer priced it to him like this: Basic cow, $200; two-tone exterior, $45; extra stomach, $75; product storage compartment, $60; dispensing device, four spigots at $10 each, $40. Genuine cowhide upholstery, $125; dual horns, $15; automatic fly swatter, $35. Total, $595.

Rusty Wright and Linda Raney Wright

•••

Daniel Webster was once bested by one of the farmers of his native state. He had been hunting at some distance from his inn, and rather than make the long trip back, he approached a farmhouse some considerable time after dark and pounded on the door. An upstairs window was raised and the farmer, with head thrust out, called, "What do you want?"

"I want to spend the night here," said Webster.

"All right. Stay there," said the farmer. Down went the window.

Bob Phillips

•••

www.CartoonStock.com

PRAIRIE FARMER

The Kranses were the nearest kinfolk we had in America except for the Holmes family in Galesburg. When John and Lena Krans bought their farm in the early 1870s, they worked from daylight to dark eight or nine months of the year till at last the mortgages were paid off. They had help from neighbors in getting in their crops and in turn helped the neighbors. The Kranses became part of the land they owned. Their feet wore paths that didn't change over the years—in the cow pasture with a small creek winding over it, the corn and oat fields, the vegetable garden, the potato patch. John Krans was a landsman, his thoughts never far from his land, the animals, the crops. He could talk about *hastarna*, meaning "horses," so to my mind he seemed part horse.

He was a medium-sized man, but he had a loose easy way of carrying his shoulders with his head flung back so he gave the impression of being a big man. His eyes had gleam and his lips had a smile you could see through the beard. Even amid the four walls of a room his head, hair, and beard seemed to be in a high wind. When I sat on his knee and ran my five-year-old hand around in his beard, he called me *min lille gosse* ("my little boy") and there was a ripple of laughter and love in it. He read his Bible and sometimes a newspaper, though most often he liked to read the land and the sky, the ways of horses and corn. He wasn't an arguing man, except that with a plow he could argue against stubborn land and with strong hands on leather reins he could argue with runaway horses.

Not often on Sunday did he miss hitching a horse to a light wagon and taking the family to the Lutheran Church a mile or two away. I doubt whether he ever listened to a preacher who had less fear and more faith than he had. I have sometimes thought that John Krans pictured God as a farmer whose chores were endless and inconceivable, that in this world and in worlds beyond God planted and tended and reaped His crops in mysterious ways past human understanding.

Carl Sandburg

FUN

We Swanbergs are just regular folks. When I was growing up, we didn't always have a whole bunch of money, but that was all right. We learned to do things that were fun but didn't cost us anything.

For example, we'd load up the family in our '49 Ford and drive from our country town down to Congress Avenue, the main street of Austin, Texas. Then we'd park in front of the

Paramount Theater. We never went to the movie; we just watched the people lined up to go. It didn't cost us a thing. People would line up to buy their tickets, go in, and come out—and we'd just watch.

I remember how closely my mama and daddy would watch—especially my mama, Pauline Bernadeen. She would sit there on the front seat and lean up next to Floyd—they were still in that stage of life where they liked to be close together. My older sister, Sherry Darlene, and I would sit in the back seat. (My little sister, Teri Linn, wasn't born yet.) Pauline would snuggle close to Floyd, and he'd put his arm around her. They would just look at people and have the time of their lives.

Once Mama said, "Look, Floyd, look. Would you just look at that woman? That woman in red, behind the man in the blue. Look what she has on. Can you believe she's wearing that? Could you imagine if I wore something like that? Oh my!"

I remember my daddy watching that woman walk all the way down the sidewalk. Then he looked at us kids, shaking his head sadly, and said, "Isn't that pitiful? Now that *is* pitiful." Of course, Daddy was a deacon, so he was especially picky about what people wore.

Sometimes we'd drive over to Robert Mueller Airport and do the same thing. We'd watch people get on and off the planes. We never flew in a plane, but we enjoyed just watching people get on and off and watching the planes take off and land.

I remember one time a whole family of five came off a plane. Old Floyd Leon, watching them, smacked his forehead in disbelief. "Good night, looky there! A family of five. That is ridiculous. Lord have mercy. One of them could have gone and come back and told the rest of them all about it."

We kids spent a lot of time at the automatic doors. The airport had just put in some pressure-sensitive rubber mats. When you stepped on the rubber mats, the glass door automatically opened. My sister and I could play on that thing for hours. Now I was raised a Methodist, so I knew how to shake a leg. I would just get a goin', and I'd get that door a goin' until old Floyd Leon would come over and say, "All right, get on off there now. Let some other kids play on it for a while." That was the closest we ever came to Six Flags over Texas.

I learned an important lesson from Daddy and Mama when I was young; I learned how to be happy, even when we didn't have everything we ever wanted.

Dennis Swanberg

....

A man was driving along a rural road one day when he saw a 3-legged chicken. Amazingly, he clocked the fowl running at 20 miles per hour. He accelerated to 30 mph; the chicken did too! The man sped up again; to his surprise the chicken passed him and ran down a driveway.

The man saw a farmer surrounded by dozens of 3-legged chickens. He called out, "How did you get all 3-legged chickens?"

"I started breeding them because my wife, son, and I all love to eat chicken legs."

"That's amazing!" said the driver. "How do they taste?"

"Don't know. Haven't been able to catch any of them."

Jim Kraus

An old-timer sat on the river bank, obviously awaiting a nibble, though the fishing season had not officially opened. The game warden stood behind him quietly for several minutes.

"You the game warden?" the old-timer inquired.

"Yep."

Unruffled, the old man began to move the fishing pole from side to side. Finally he lifted the line out of the water.

Pointing to a minnow wiggling on the end of the line, he said, "Just teaching him to swim."

Tal. D. Bonham

••

FAMILY TABLE

Summers in Michigan, Dad rented rows in a community garden. The farmer tilled, Dad planted, another watered, we weeded and God gave the increase. Mama spent many days in a steamy kitchen putting up that increase in canning jars. We carried jars from the storeroom in the basement, washed them in hot soapy water, then later carried them filled, back down, arranging them in rows on the storeroom shelves.

I loved the garden, especially the corn rows, so long the ends seemed to meet and touch. The corn stalks were tall enough to make shady lanes to run down. I'm afraid Kent and I weren't much help. We played happily in the magical green aisles, chasing each other up and back until we tired. Then we sat in the delicious shade and played in the sandy dirt. Dad checked the corn often, and when he found it just right, we picked bushels to take home to feed to the Matic Seal pressure canner.

You may think that there were only two times when Jesus fed the multitude (Matthew 14:14 and Matthew 15:32), but there you would be wrong! Multitudes were fed at our house on a regular basis (often seeming like a miracle to us). On a summer evening a Volkswagen busload of cousins might turn in the drive. Mama would send one of us for a couple of jars of tomatoes and corn from the basement to add to the soup, along with a few potatoes and everyone would be fed!

A warm Sunday afternoon would bring a carload or two of church friends, lured to the country by the promise of a swim in the river, maybe followed by a slice of icy watermelon Dad had tied a rope to and lowered down into the river to cool; or maybe a bowl of sweet ice cream fresh from the cranker.

We saw pictures of the starving children in Ethiopia. We worried about them and prayed for them, although we could not know what starving was. We did our part by collecting for UNICEF every October. With our little milk cartons we went door to door asking the neighbors to give for the hungry. "The hungry" were not us. We had plenty to eat always.

Mama raised chickens one year. She hated chickens. We children thought the chickens were great. We liked to feed them and gather the eggs. Mama despised them. She thought they stank. They were a nuisance. They further would not oblige her by laying their eggs in the nesting boxes. Shortly following an episode in which little brother Fred, was chased and pecked by a mean old rooster, Kent and I were sent out to gather eggs. Finding only three in the nest boxes, we filled our basket with pearly whites from the woods.

Mama's cake batter was ruined by a horrible stinky rotten egg. That was the last straw. Mama made those feathers fly! She chased those hens down and she wrung necks until she'd exhausted herself. She and Dad spent all that evening cleaning chickens and Mama spent all the next day canning chicken, on the bone in half gallon Mason jars.

Many a hungry multitude was fed Texas-style chicken and dumplings at our table that winter. Sickly friends were resuscitated with bowls of hearty chicken noodle soup from Mama's stores. On winter days when the snow was too deep for us to walk home from school for lunch, we carried hot chicken soup in our lunch box thermoses.

Often Mama rummaged up meals for strangers that Dad picked up and carried home. One night late in a snow storm, Dad came in with a family he had found in a broken down vehicle by the side of the road. The family had an infant, a little girl with a head grotesquely misshapen. She had encephalitis, water on the brain. They were hungry, cold, terrified, trying desperately to get the baby to a hospital. After warming them and feeding them, Dad took them on into the city. We never heard from them afterward and often wondered if the baby lived.

Traveling evangelists and preachers often found a chair at our table as well. I especially recall one from Texas, with a lovely southern drawl, who spent an afternoon picknicking with us at the tree farm. Mama had fixed her specialty, fried chicken. We feasted on chicken, beans, bread and butter, potato salad, corn on the cob, all washed down with fresh cold milk. For dessert there were ice cream cones filled with chocolate pudding and decorated with sprinkles.

Kent and I polished off our puddings and then helped ourselves to a second one before running off to explore. The adults were busy talking about Texas, where Mama and Dad had lived when they first married. Kent and I went back and listened for a while, then ate a third cone. All was well until the preacher went to get his dessert. "Oh, no," he croaked, peering into the box, "The puddings are all gone! I was so looking forward to eating me one! Why, I could jeeeest bawl!"

"I could jeeeest bawl!" became our family's by-line for any disappointment in life. It helped us laugh through rough spots we faced now and then, and to keep our chins up.

Elece Hollis

PASS THE WHIPPED CREAM

It's a wonder I can still look a strawberry straight in the eye! I must have picked millions of them in the summers of my childhood, bending over under the hot sun to earn the princely sum of two cents per quart. There were not many paying jobs for kids in those days, so every one of us put in time in the strawberry patch. We probably ate two berries for every ten that we picked, but our real motive was income—cash on hand for the Fourth of July carnival.

Every year there was a Strawberry Festival in Bayfield on the Fourth of July. The Women's Auxiliary of the American Legion would set up a tent where they served nothing but strawberry shortcake—homemade cake, fresh berries, and fresh whipped cream. It cost a quarter to get in, and then you could have all the strawberry shortcake you wanted. To me it was sheer heaven, although I recall that more than once I left that tent with a powerful feeling of nausea.

Dad just loved the Fourth of July. He always saw to it that there were plenty of firecrackers on hand, the louder the better. Dad would get up very early, about five o'clock, and he would set off several loud bombs to start the celebrating. The kids in the neighborhood loved all the excitement, and the neighbors never complained, but our dog nearly went crazy. He would hide under my bed for the entire day and night; maybe he thought the world was coming to an end, or maybe the sharp explosions hurt his ears. Anyway, we never saw the dog again until July fifth.

I remember how proud Dad was of the medals he had earned during his service in the Spanish-American War. Every Fourth of July he would get them out of the box in his dresser and pin them all on his best white shirt.

There was always a picnic around the Fourth of July, even though it took some incredible planning to get us all together.

All my brothers and sisters came, even the married ones, and everybody brought carloads of food. Sometimes we picknicked on the shore of Lake Superior and sometimes at a small, inland lake or on a river bank.

My brothers and I did a lot of trout fishing during the summer, whenever we weren't lined up for farm chores. Our favorite spots were the streams that empty into Lake Superior, and if we were really lucky we'd bring home enough rainbow, brook, or German browns for our family dinner.

Sometimes Ed, Milt, and I would go fishing early in the morning. If the fish were biting and we caught our limit, we'd fix a shore lunch. After we cleaned the fish, we would wrap them in maple leaves and then in red clay. One of us would build a fire, and we baked the fish until they were succulent, steaming, and delicious.

It could be that we enjoyed fishing so much because we had so little time for it. There was a lot of work to be done on the farm in the summer, and we all had to do our share. Sometimes I used to think that "summer" and "haying" were pretty much the same thing. Our hay crop had to be mowed, raked, stacked, and hauled to the barn. It was hot, dusty work, and it was also physically exhausting. Everything was done by hand; the hay was not rolled or baled as it is nowadays.

Once the hay was mowed, it had to dry, so we stacked it into long rows across the field. Then we made hayshocks out of the rows, building them so that the rain would run off. We continually worried that it would rain before we could get the hay into the barn.

The hayshocks were always small enough so that two people could lift them with pitchforks onto the hay wagon. My brothers and I always competed with one another to see which one of us was strong enough to lift a hayshock all by himself. Our shoulder muscles ached, but it was a matter of honor to try and accomplish that feat of sheer strength.

Unfortunately, the hayshocks were ideal hiding places for snakes and mice. You never knew when a mouse would run down your arm, or when a snake would drop out of the hay and slither across your foot. The mice never bothered me, but I had a strong aversion to snakes and I was scared to death every time one popped out of the hay.

Once the hay arrived at the barn, someone had to stay inside the barn and keep moving the hay toward the back to make room for more. As the youngest child, I inherited that less-than-pleasant job. While the others got to work outdoors, I was stuck in that smelly barn where the temperature must have stayed well over 100 degrees. The hay was dry and dusty and prickly, and my arms and face were covered with sweat. Never did a glass of lemonade taste as wonderful as it did when I finally got out of that barn!

My brothers and I spent hours every summer tramping through the woods looking for berries. We would take some of Ma's berry baskets or a couple old pails along and try to fill them with blueberries and blackberries, chokecherries or pin cherries. And although we tried to be very nonchalant, every one of us was terrified that we'd come eyeball to eyeball with a foraging bear who was also in the market for some fresh fruit.

Some of our courage went into every jar of jam that Ma ever made. And some of our back strain went into every piece of strawberry shortcake we devoured. Even so, my favorite dessert remains, to this day, strawberry shortcake.

Bea Bourgeois

•••

A man is driving up a steep, narrow mountain road. A woman is driving down the same road. As they pass each other the woman leans out the

window and yells, "PIG!!" The man immediately leans out his window and yells out, "IDIOT!!" They each continue on their way, and as the man rounds the next corner, he crashes into a pig in the middle of the road.

Lowell D. Streiker

A MAN CAN'T JUST SIT AROUND

I suppose most people have dreams, but how many people actually turn their dreams into reality? Larry Walters is among the relatively few who have. His story is true, though you may find it hard to believe.

Larry was a truck driver, but his lifelong dream was to fly. When he graduated from high school, he joined the air force in hopes of becoming a pilot. Unfortunately, poor eyesight disqualified him. So when he finally left the service, he had to satisfy himself with watching others fly the fighter jets that crisscrossed the skies over his backyard. As he sat there in his lawn chair, he dreamed about the magic of flying.

Then one day, Larry Walters got an idea. He went down to the local Army-Navy Surplus Store and bought a tank of helium and forty-five weather balloons. These were not your brightly colored party balloons; these were heavy-duty spheres measuring more than four feet across when fully inflated.

Back in his yard, Larry used straps to attach the balloons to his lawn chair, the kind you might have in your own backyard. He anchored the chair to the bumper of his jeep and inflated the balloons with helium. Then he packed some sandwiches and drinks and loaded a BB gun, figuring he could pop a few of those balloons when it was time to return to earth.

His preparations complete, Larry Walters sat in his chair and cut the anchoring cord. His plan was to lazily float back down to terra firma. But things didn't quite work out that way.

When Larry cut the cord, he didn't float lazily up; he shot up as if fired from a cannon! Nor did he go up a couple hundred feet. He climbed and climbed until he finally leveled off at eleven thousand feet! At that height, he could hardly risk deflating any of the balloons, lest he unbalance the load and really experience flying! So he stayed up there, sailing around for fourteen hours, totally at a loss as to how to get down.

Eventually, Larry drifted into the approach corridor for Los Angeles International Airport. A Pan Am pilot radioed the tower about passing a guy in a lawn chair at eleven thousand feet with a gun in his lap. (Now there's a conversation I'd have given anything to have heard!)

LAX is right on the ocean, and you may know that at nightfall, the winds on the coast begin to change. So, as dusk fell, Larry began drifting out to sea. At that point, the navy dispatched a helicopter to rescue him. But the rescue team had a hard time getting to him, because the draft from their propeller kept pushing his home-made contraption farther and farther away. Eventually they were able to hover over him and drop a rescue line with which they gradually hauled him back to earth.

As soon as Larry hit the ground he was arrested. But as he was being led away in handcuffs, a television reporter called out, "Mr. Walters, why'd you do it?"

Larry stopped, eyed the man, then replied nonchalantly, "A man can't just sit around."

Chip MacGregor

THROUGH THE ROCKY ROAD

My three country-girl cousins were the middle batch of nine children belonging to my mom's eldest sister, Lucille, and her husband, Al. They lived in a wonderful old house down a country lane.

My sister and I loved spending the night at their house. The five of us girls would sleep crosswise on the double bed that the three middle cousins shared—with one of us always having to hold onto the edge of the bed to keep from falling out. We'd whisper and giggle about boys, lipstick, and The Monkees long into the night—until even sweet, good-natured Uncle Al hollered up the stairs at us to be quiet.

During the day, we'd pick berries, play hide-and-seek in the nearby apple orchard, or sometimes lock their brother—my cousin Henry, who was a year younger than me—in the neighbor's outhouse. (Although my cousins had indoor plumbing, it broke a lot, so we'd have to use the neighbor's outhouse.)

Those were the days.

One winter day stands out especially clear in my memory.

We'd trooped down the street to the local pond, having fun slipping and sliding across the ice in our red rubber boots, when all of a sudden (just like the young Harry Bailey in *It's a Wonderful Life*), crack! The ice broke beneath me, and I fell into the frigid water.

It wasn't Jimmy Stewart who saved me but rather Peppy, my cousins' beloved collie-mix, who gently pulled me out of the pond gasping and sputtering—and with a couple of minnows swimming in my boots.

No wonder I'm not a fan of water sports.

Yet this didn't dampen my enthusiasm for the country life.

A tomboy through and through, I loved making tree forts with my cousins, jumping in piles of crunchy leaves, or sneaking apples from the orchard down the street. My Aunt Lucille always bought bushels of apples from the orchard owner—which more than made up for the few we snuck now and then, but as a kid, it was so much more fun to pick the most shiny, perfect apple we wanted from the tree ourselves. We'd also have contests for who built the best miniature outhouse. One of us—I can't remember who after all these years, but I think it was my cousin Kathy—made a really great one out of a deck of cards.

Often, we would roller-skate downstairs in the basement, since there weren't any cement sidewalks nearby to practice on. Other times, in an inspired burst of helpfulness, we'd wash and wax the dining room floor for Aunt Lucille by skating around it on rags in the wee hours of the morning. Then there was the time Uncle Al brought home an old Jeep from which he removed the engine and the wheels. We kids made it into a playhouse, complete with curtains and furniture.

Now that's what you call a mobile home.

I started thinking about all this country-girl stuff recently because my friend Jan—a true country girl if I've ever met one—invited me to accompany her on a "writing retreat" to her snug little cabin in a beautiful pine forest in Northern California.

My first clue that I had turned in my tomboy badge for

good came when I stepped out of the car and felt my white sandals sink into the dusty dirt.

E-yew. I just hate it when my feet get dirty. Don't you?

But I bravely resisted the urge to wash them the second we entered the cabin, reminding myself that I wasn't in Kansas anymore, so I shouldn't expect a gleaming yellow brick road.

Inside the adorable cabin was a loft—just like the one where Mary and Laura Ingalls used to sleep! How exciting. Only problem was that in all my Little House dreams, I was a pigtailed little girl happily scampering up the steep ladder to the loft . . .

I haven't been pigtailed or little in years.

And I can't recall the last time I scampered.

Petite country-girl Jan saved the day, however, by announcing that she'd sleep in the loft and I could take the downstairs guest room.

Heavy sigh of relief.

To show my gratitude, I made dinner that first night.

Okay, so it wasn't Ma Ingalls' beef stew and flaky homemade biscuits, but I'm willing to bet that my pasta with sauce from a jar and store-bought rolls could easily rival her cooking any day.

Who says I'm not a country girl?

Jan.

Especially after we tried to eat outside the second night and got swarmed by "meat bees" (that looked suspiciously like hornets to me). Jan calmly swatted them away and continued talking and eating, while I edged closer to the screen door, saying, "I think it might be a little bit cooler inside . . ."

Later that night as we were typing away on our trusty laptops, several gnats, lured by the glow of my computer, began hovering around my face. I'd swat at them and continue typing, but pretty soon my punctuation began to get messed up. I couldn't tell if the mark on my paper was a comma or a gnat.

One more country-girl strike against me.

I simply don't like bugs (or any kind of critter—birds, bats, mosquitoes) flying in front of my face.

Which is kind of a problem in the great outdoors.

Guess I just have to face the fact that the terrible tomboy has grown into a big W.U.S.S. with a capital W (Woman Unable to Survive in the Sticks).

But I'm still not willing to concede that I'm not a country girl. I really, really do love the great outdoors and all its beauty.

As long as I can enjoy it from the comfort of my indoor armchair.

Laura Jensen Walker

THE HOME TOWN

It doesn't matter much be its building great or small,
The home town, the home town, is the best town, after all.
The cities of the millions have the sun and stars above,
But they lack the friendly faces of the few you've learned to love,
And with all their pomp of riches and with all their teeming throngs,
The heart of man is rooted in the town where he belongs.

There are places good to visit, there are cities fair to see,
There are haunts of charm and beauty where at times it's good to be,
But the humblest little hamlet sings a melody to some,
And no matter where they travel it is calling them to come;
Though cities rise to greatness and are gay with gaudy dress,
There is something in the home town which no other towns possesss.

The home town has a treasure which the distance cannot gain,
It is there the hearts are kindest, there the gentlest friends remain;
It is there a mystic something seems to permeate the air
To set the weary wanderer to wishing he were there;
And be it great or humble, it still holds mankind in thrall,
For the home town, the home town, is the best town after all.

Edgar A. Guest

Acknowledgments

All material that originally appeared in *Daily Guideposts* and *Guideposts* magazine is reprinted with permission. Copyright by Guideposts, Carmel, New York 10512. All rights reserved.

Anderson, Mac. *A Smile Increases Your Face Value.* Lombard, IL: Great Quotations, 1991.

Bolton, Martha. *When the Going Gets Tough, the Tough Start Laughing.* Chicago, IL: Moody, 1996.

Bonham, Tal D. *The Treasury of Clean Jokes.* Nashville, TN: Broadman & Holman, 1997.

Bottke, Allison Gappa. *More God Allows U-Turns.* Uhrichsville, OH: Promise Press, an imprint of Barbour Publishing, 2001.

Brownlow, Leroy. *Let's Laugh a Little.* Fort Worth, TX: Brownlow, 1993. Used by permission.

Dickson, Paul. *The Official Rules at Home.* New York: Walker and Company, 1996.

Reprinted from *At the Corner of Mundane and Grace.* Copyright ©1999 by Chris Fabry. Used by permission of WaterBrook Press, Colorado Springs, CO. All rights reserved.

Freeman, Becky. *Help! I'm Turning Into My Mother.* Eugene, OR: Harvest House, 2002. Used by permission. www.harvesthousepublishers.com.

———. *Lemonade Laughter and Laid-Back Joy.* Eugene, OR: Harvest House, 2001. Used by permission. www.harvesthousepublishers.com.

Gilbert, Rachel St. John. *Wake Up Laughing* published by Barbour Publishing, Inc. Uhrichsville, OH: Barbour, 2004. Used by permission.

Green, Michael. *Illustrations for Biblical Preaching.* Grand Rapids, MI: Baker, 1989.

Grizzard, Lewis. *Chili Dawgs Always Bark at Night.* New York: Random House, 1965.

Hafer, Todd and Jedd. *Mischief From the Back Pew.* Grand Rapids, MI: Bethany House, 2003.

Hale, Leon. *Turn South at the Second Bridge.* New York: Doubleday, a division of Random House, 1965.

Hollingsworth, Amy. *The Simple Faith of Mr. Rogers.* Nashville: Integrity Publishers, 2005.

Hollingsworth, Mary. "The Porch Light's On. Who Died?" Administered by Shady Oaks Studio, 1507 Shirley Way, Bedford, TX 76022. Used by permission.

———. "She Dade." Administered by Shady Oaks Studio, 1507 Shirley Way, Bedford, TX 76022. Used by permission.

———. "You Can't Do That." Administered by Shady Oaks Studio, 1507 Shirley Way, Bedford, TX 76022. Used by permission.

———. "Delivering the US Mail." Administered by Shady Oaks Studio, 1507 Shirley Way, Bedford, TX 76022. Used by permission.

Holmes, Marjorie. *Love and Laughter.* New York: Bantam, a division of Random House, Inc., 1967.

Keillor, Garrison. *The Prairie Home Companion Joke Book.* Saint Paul, MN: Minnesota Public Radio, 1996.

Kraus, James. *Bloopers, Blunders, Quips, Jokes, and Quotes.* Wheaton, IL: Tyndale, 2005. Used by permission.

Linkletter, Art. *Oops! Or, Life's Awful Moments.* New York: Doubleday, a division of Random House, Inc., 1967.

"A Man Can't Just Sit Around" by Chip MacGregor. Quoted from *Standing Together.* Gresham, OR: Vision House, 1995.

McPherson, John. *Close to Home.* Used by permission.

Myers, James. *A Treasury of Medical Humor.* South Bend, IN: And Books, 1993. Used by permission.

Phillips, Bob. *The Ultimate Joke Book.* Eugene, OR: Harvest House, 2002. Used by permission. www.harvesthousepublishers.com.

———. *The World's Greatest Collection of Clean Jokes.* Eugene, OR: Harvest House, 1998. Used by permission. www.harvesthousepublishers.com.

———. *Phillips Book of Great Thoughts and Funny Sayings.* Wheaton, IL: Tyndale, 1993.

———. *The Best Ever Book of Good Clean Jokes.* Eugene, OR: Harvest House, 1998. Used by permission. www.harvesthousepublishers.com.

———. *Bob Phillip's Encyclopedia of Good Clean Jokes.* Eugene, OR: Harvest House, 1992. Used by permission. www.harvesthousepublishers.com.

Pierce, Chonda. *It's Always Darkest Before the Fun Comes Up.* Grand Rapids, MI: Zondervan, 1998. Used by permission of The Zondervan Corporation.

Smith, John William. *Rocking Chair Tales.* West Monroe, LA: Howard, 2005.

Stibbe, Mark and J. John. *A Box of Delights.* Oxford, UK: Monarch, 2001.

——. *A Barrel of Fun.* Oxford, UK: Monarch, 2003.

Streiker, Lowell D. *Nelson's Big Book of Laughter.* Nashville, TN: Thomas Nelson, 2000. Used by permission of Thomas Nelson, Inc.

——.*Encyclopedia of Humor.* Peabody, MA: Hendrickson, 1998.

Swanberg, Dennis. *Swan's Soup and Salad.* West Monroe, LA: Howard, 1999.

From the book *The Mammoth Book of Zingers, Quips, and One-Liners* Copyright ©2004. Appears by permission of the publisher, Carroll & Graf, A Division of Avalon Publishing Group, Inc.

Walker, Laura Jensen. *Through the Rocky Road and Into the Rainbow Sherbet: Hope and Laughter for Life's Hard Licks.* Grand Rapids, MI: Fleming H. Revell, a division of Baker Book House, 2002.

My Love is Free . . . but the rest of me don't come cheap, P.S. Wall, ©1997. Reprinted by permission of Rutledge Hill Press, a division of Thomas Nelson, Inc., Nashville, Tennessee. All rights reserved.

World's Best Bathroom Book. ©2000. Used with permission by Cook Communications Ministries. May not be further reproduced. To order, www.cookministries.com. All rights reserved.

Wright, Rusty and Linda Raney. *500 Clean Jokes and Humorous Stories* published by Barbour Publishing, Inc. Uhrichsville, OH: Barbour, 1985. Used by permission.

Ziglar, Zig. *Over the Top.* Nashville: Thomas Nelson, 1994.

A Note from the Editors

This original book was created by the Books and Inspirational Media Division of Guideposts, the world's leading inspirational publisher. Founded in 1945 by Dr. Norman Vincent Peale and his wife Ruth Stafford Peale, Guideposts helps people from all walks of life achieve their maximum personal and spiritual potential. Guideposts is committed to communicating positive, faith-filled principles for people everywhere to use in successful daily living.

Other publications include award-winning magazines like *Guideposts, Angels on Earth, Sweet 16,* and *Positive Thinking,* best-selling books, and outreach services that demonstrate what can happen when faith and positive thinking are applied to day-to-day life.

For more information, visit us online at www.guideposts.org, call (800) 431-2344 or write Guideposts, 39 Seminary Hill Road, Carmel, New York 10512.